NO LONGER A VICTIM

Answers for the Pain Inside

NO LONGER A VICTIM

Answers for the Pain Inside

Burton Stokes

&

Lynn Lucas

Edited by *Betty Stokes*

Destiny Image Publishers
P.O. Box 310
Shippensburg, PA 17257

**"Speaking to the Purposes of God for this Generation
and for the Generations to Come"**

ISBN 0-914903-72-1
Library of Congress Catalog Card Number 88-51828

For Worldwide Distribution
Printed in the U.S.A.

First Printing: 1988
Second Printing: 1995

Destiny Image books are available through these fine distributors outside the United States:

Christian Growth, Inc.
Jalan Kilang-Timor, Singapore 0315

Successful Christian Living
Capetown, Rep. of South Africa

Lifestream
Nottingham, England

Vision Resources
Ponsonby, Auckland, New Zealand

Rhema Ministries Trading
Randburg, South Africa

WA Buchanan Company
Geebung, Queensland, Australia

Salvation Book Centre
Petaling, Jaya, Malaysia

Word Alive
Niverville, Manitoba, Canada

Inside the U.S., call toll free to order:
1-800-722-6774

DEDICATION

To all the pastors, ministers, counselors, concerned lay persons and compassionate workers in the Kingdom of God who are laboring in the fields and vineyards of the Master to bring the fruit of the Gospel of Jesus Christ to damaged lives and suffering people. May this book be a true help to shine the light of the Gospel into the dark and hidden places that truth and light, mercy and grace may come to the victims of the one who has come to "steal, kill and destroy."

Our prayer is that the information in this book will be a help and an encouragement to you as you labor in His love and that the Holy Spirit of the living God will guide and direct you in bringing the healing and delivering power of the Cross to those who are sick in soul and body. To God be the Glory!

ACKNOWLEDGMENT

We are deeply grateful to God for the members of Living Faith Church, San Antonio, Texas, and Fountainhead Congregation, Elwood, Long Island, New York. They have lovingly supported the writing of this book and have prayed for and encouraged us during all of the difficult times until completion of the book was accomplished. Further thanks go to the leaders of both churches who covered ministry responsibilities, thus freeing us to write.

It takes many people to see a book come into existence and we would like to personally thank the following people:

To our editor, Betty Stokes, goes our love and appreciation for her willingness to work long and hard hours to see this book a reality. [Betty, this work would have been a nightmare had it not been for your dedication and hard work to edit and translate my written words into understandable spelling and grammar. Thank you for what must have seemed like an unending task. — Lynn]

We appreciate the willingness of Susan Weddington to stay up nights to ensure manuscripts were justified and printed in time to meet deadlines.

Our thanks to Kathy Petraitis for proofreading and editing portions of the manuscript and for her help at times when so much had to be done so quickly.

TABLE OF CONTENTS

FOREWORD

Antiquity has forwarded to us the comprehension that "to realize the worth of the anchor, we need to feel the stress of the storm." *No Longer a Victim* is a book about the mounting intensity of hurricane force storms that rob the soul of its rest, mar the human personality and leave personhood and self worth in a broken stupor. In all this, there is the quiet assertion that the anchor resoundingly holds. Christ is the answer and every demonic force has been conquered by Him.

Stokes and Lucas couple a keen insight in human problems with an equally refined theology that finds *No Longer a Victim* a welcome addition to the caring person's library. The authors, both counselors and pastors, share practical truth that brings the theoretical off its lofted position and makes it wrestle in the arenas where we live.

Faith is always deserving the leash of a sober mind. This book brings faith and sobriety to the altar and insures a dynamic marriage of the two.

God and His Word are the foundation on which the text *No Longer a Victim* stands.

Dr. Sam Sasser

Chapter 1

INTRODUCTION

The purpose of this book is to share the results of years of study and ministerial experience in the hope that what we have learned will benefit others. Nothing learned through experience in the Holy Spirit School of Ministry is proprietary, and those things which are revealed belong to us and our children forever, but the secret things belong to God.

While we cannot write the final chapter and say, "That's it, there is no more!" we believe we must share what we have acquired, hoping and praying it will be a blessing to the many who are in bondage to they know not what but, nevertheless, they know is real.

In the medical field, results of early experiments and pioneer efforts are reported and circulated, not to fuel the egos of the investigators, but to provide help, hope and promise to others who may be pondering and probing like problems.

With the advent of the classical Pentecostal movement, and more recently the neo-Pentecostal movement of the 20th century, there has been a major shift in Christendom from a mystical and intellectual religion to one in which the experience of Christ is far more personal and tangible. With the coming of the Holy Spirit in power, there is an increasing awareness and sensitivity to the spirit world. People are beginning to see there are real causes for problems which do not originate in the natural realm but in the supernatural.

While most of Christendom is confined to the "Western mind-set" fashioned by the Reformation, and the philosophies of Rationalism and the "Age of Enlightenment," a significant segment of Christianity today is "charismatic" in nature, even if by widely varying degrees.

The purpose of this book is not to debate the theological definition of Holy Spirit baptism or even glossolalia. We are bypassing the academic hair-splitters and going directly into the laboratory where things happen, and one quickly learns that academic theology does not always provide practical answers. It is often necessary to discard preconceived notions of the way things are and to return to a more literal interpretation of the Bible. We have long ago learned that the Bible teaches that God has eminently practical answers to the problems of this life if we will only open our eyes and our ears while we study the Word, and if we fervently pray for His infinite wisdom and guidance.

The purpose of this book is not to debate the existence and operation of the Devil nor the presence of demons in our world. This book will be of little or no practical value to you if you cannot accept these things as real. In a doctor's office some patients may not believe in the existence and prevalence of germs, bacteria and viruses because they are not discerned by the senses, but the doctor is not going to debate the issue before attempting diagnosis and treatment.

Suffice it to say, the only reliable textbook that provides definitive answers to spiritual problems is the Holy Bible. Whatever our experience, we continue to refer to this bulwark and foundation of truth for guidance.

For years, medical science has recognized the connection between the body and the soul as it relates to health. We have heard various figures as to how many illnesses today have their origins not in the body, but in the soul. The terms "psychosomatic illness" and "stress-induced illness" have been around for a long time, and the medical profession clearly recognizes the connection. Some researchers say that the percentage of patients in hospitals and doctors' waiting rooms who suffer from psychosomatic or stress-induced illnesses may be as high as 80%.

If the sickness of the soul affects such a high percentage of patients, would it not be incumbent upon us to concentrate on the causes and cures of "soul problems"? Would not the body then respond accordingly? The dramatic increase of social problems in our society is related to "soul problems" of the individual. The many psychiatrists, psychologists and counselors who are attempting to deal with the psychoses and lesser maladjustment problems of individuals are a reflection of the extent of the pervasive malaise of souls.

Everyone is searching for answers, for inner peace and contentment, but precious few find lasting relief from the torture and bondage from within. Even among Christians, the rate of psychosomatic and stress-related illnesses is only slightly lower than among non-Christians. They all are searching for the key that will unlock the prison within. Some search for it in drugs and alcohol, some on the therapist's couch, some in following an Eastern guru and some in other avenues. While some have found a degree of symptomatic relief through these avenues, the bondage remains that makes the individual know in his heart of hearts that he is a prisoner still, and a victim of an unseen oppression. The Gospel of Jesus Christ is that He came to reconcile us to God and to save us from our enemies. He came that we might be free, and, if the Son sets you free, then you are free indeed.

It is our sincere desire that what is presented in this book will open the doors and windows of the prison to let in light and air in order that the prisoners will see a Great Light and that there will be hope, deliverance and healing for their souls and bodies.

Chapter 2

REALITY

In Romans 1:20, the apostle Paul, writing under the inspiration of the Holy Spirit, declared:

For the invisible things of Him from the creation of the world are clearly seen, being understood by the things that are made, even His eternal power and Godhead;...

And then in II Corinthians 4:18 we read:

While we look not at the things which are seen, but at the things which are not seen: for the things which are seen are temporal; but the things which are not seen are eternal.

The Bible clearly sets forth the existence of the unseen universe and declares the temporal and transitory nature of the physical. Jesus Himself declared, *"Heaven and earth shall pass away but My Word shall never pass away."* In another place He said that *"Not one jot nor one tittle shall fail till all be fulfilled."* In Luke 16:17, Jesus said that *"...it is easier for heaven and earth to pass, than for one tittle of the law to fail."* Therefore, we may move with confidence of the certainty and permanence of spiritual laws and principles which are more durable and immutable than the natural.

If we then accept that the physical world is but a vague representation of the spiritual, unseen realm, we must deal with spiritual laws as well as physical laws, the spiritual laws being above and eminent over the physical. We are spiritual beings, therefore subject to spiritual laws, as certainly and immutably as we are as physical beings subject to physical laws.

Laws of dynamics, gravity, light, etc. remain constant, consistent and universal throughout all creation. It is on this very fundamental truth that our modern science and technology rest. We cannot annul the law of gravity. We can only invoke a higher law such as aerodynamics. We do not make gravity cease to exert its pull upon us when we are at 30,000 feet in a modern jet. We are merely using another principle, another law, to temporarily overcome the effects of gravity. Should aerodynamic integrity be compromised, the consequence of gravity would be certain and predictable. So it is with spiritual laws. We can cooperate with the physical laws to our good, ignore or violate them to our peril. So too, we can cooperate with the spiritual laws and prosper or we can ignore and violate them to our hurt.

We read in Romans 8:2, *"For the law of the Spirit of life in Christ Jesus hath made me free from the law of sin and death."* As long as we remain operating in the law of the Spirit of life in Christ Jesus (a "higher" law), we are free from the law of sin and death. Although the law of the Spirit of life in Christ Jesus is available to us, God did not repeal the law of sin and death. If we violate the law of the Spirit of life, the law of sin and death takes over!

To assist in dealing with spiritual reality, we need a "model" which we can see, touch, taste, smell and hear. The physical universe is given as that model. *"The things not seen (spiritual) are understood by the things which are seen (physical)"* (Rom. 1:20).

The physical world teaches eloquently about the spirit world. Jesus used innumerable examples of nature to illustrate the Kingdom of God. He spoke and taught in parables, only some of which are recorded in the Gospels. Many times it is recorded that Jesus said, *"The Kingdom of God (or Heaven) is like ...."* and then proceeded to give an example from nature to illustrate the spiritual principle. This was not a simple, poetic expression to communicate to an agrarian culture. He spoke to everyone, both Jew and Gentile, rich and poor, publican and beggar, physician and scholar, and to illiterate fishermen. It was not just a case of using universal symbolism, it was drawing parallels between the real and the shadow. Every example of nature had its counterpart in the spiritual: seed, fruit, sheaves, progressive development, etc. It was neither accident nor coincidence that Jesus used these examples. He created the physical universe, established it, and upholds all the laws of that universe by the word of His power. He created grass bearing seed because there is a spiritual reality of which that is but a shadow. He created the fruit of trees because there is a spiritual law therein reflected. Why do we think it strange that God says in Hebrews 2:2-3:

> *For if the word spoken by angels was stedfast and every transgression and disobedience received a just recompense of reward; How shall we escape, if we neglect so great salvation; . . .*

Chapter 3

SPIRITUAL CONFLICT

Until the coming of Jesus Christ almost 2,000 years ago, there had not been a man on earth for 4,000 years who had authority over the prince of the power of the air and all of his minions. In Genesis 1:26, God said, *"Let us make man in our image and give them dominion over the works of our hands."* Adam was given the command to subdue the earth and rule over it. These are terms of government. It must be remembered that Adam was the only man on the face of the earth at the time God gave him that command. (It was not until after the fall that God revealed the tension that would arise between the man and his wife.)

The command to subdue the earth implies the existence of something which is in opposition to God's rule and order. If there was nothing in conflict with, and in opposition to, God's order, there would be no need to exercise power and authority to bring it into submission. The immediate question is, what was it that Adam was to subdue and rule over ("Adam" includes both the man and the woman because God called *their* name Adam)?

In the opening verse of Genesis 3, we see the very first statement that God made about the serpent who is the manifestation of Satan. *"Now the serpent was more subtil than any beast of the field which the LORD God had made . . . ."* The serpent was in the garden. Adam had authority over him and could have told him to get out of the garden and the serpent would have obeyed. By getting into a dialog with the serpent, Adam and Eve opened the door to deception. By listening to the crafty serpent, they decided that they wanted to live apart from God's authority, chose their own wills over God's will, and by transgression fell. In the fall of Adam, he lost his authority over the spirits, and the war that began in Heaven long before God said "Let there be light" came to the garden of Eden. Adam, made in the image and likeness of God, was the first casualty.

One of the most important truths that can be learned is that man was created for the purpose of dominion. The first statement in the Bible that concerns man says that. Genesis 1:26 states:

> *And God said, Let us make man in our image, after our likeness: and let them have dominion over the fish of the sea, and over the fowl of the air, and over the cattle, and over all the earth, and over every creeping thing that creepeth upon the earth.*

It should be no surprise that there is within man a propensity to dominate. It was put there by God and of itself is not evil. It is the perversion of that drive that is evil. In the list of things over which God gave man dominion, man or woman is not listed. We are "fellow laborers," not masters and slaves. The task that God gave Adam was clear, and Adam knew very well what was expected of him. The Bible tells us that God breathed the breath of life into Adam and that he became a living soul.

The Hebrew word for soul is "nephesh." Anything that has life and breath is a "nephesh" by definition. "Nephesh" is also translated "life." It is equivalent to the Greek word for soul, which is "psuche," from which comes the word "psyche." The thing that made Adam different from the animals was that he was a "living soul." That is, he was a living life; a soul with "life"; a soul that had a quality of life that was separate and apart from mere biological existence. The Hebrew word for this life is "chay" and the equivalent Greek word is "zoe." Adam had two kinds of life: nephesh and chay. God said to Adam, "In the day that you eat of the fruit, you shall surely die." The day that Adam sinned, he lost his chay but still had his nephesh. The chay was the life imparted by the breath or Spirit of God. The same word is used in Daniel 12:2 and is translated "eternal life." It was on the basis of the chay or life or spirit of God that Adam had the authority over the spirits, but it was up to Adam to exercise that authority.

There is no record of anyone being delivered from an evil spirit in the Old Testament. Only briefly would the evil spirit that vexed king Saul leave when David would play the harp. The Psalmist would play and sing under the anointing of the Spirit of God and the evil spirit would be driven from his presence. Other than that, there is little that God had to say on the subject until Jesus began His public ministry. Until then, man could only avoid spiritual infection by meticulous spiritual hygiene. This is why God had to separate His people from those, such as the Canaanites, who were infected with demonic spirits.

Man's only hope to avoid being brought into captivity to evil and unclean spirits was to walk in "clean paths." Only through obedience to God would there be a protective shield around man. That is why God said that He was a shield to them that walk uprightly. National quarantine was the only recourse until the One came who had power (authority) over the unclean spirits, and the chaiyim (eternal life) which He had in Him could again be imparted to mortal (nephesh) man.

In the Gospel accounts, we see Jesus confronting the kingdom of darkness everywhere He went. Jesus came not only to proclaim the Kingdom of God, but to demonstrate it and to establish it on the earth. The battle went from a totally defensive strategy to one of offense. Confronting the works of the Devil and destroying them, Jesus healed the sick, raised the dead, and cast out demons. These were the signs of the Kingdom, all of which had been prophesied. Not only did Jesus do these things, He taught and commissioned His disciples to do the same things. In Luke 10:19, Jesus said to His disciples:

Behold, I give unto you power to tread on serpents and on scorpions, and over all the power of the enemy: and nothing shall by any means hurt you.

The Greek verb tense is: "I have given." They already had the power, and the word "power" is better translated as "authority" (in Greek, "exousia"). The disciples had authority over the "power" of the enemy. This word is the Greek word "dunamin," which is also translated "miraculous power" or "the power to perform miracles." Thus, He gave them the authority to overrule the supernatural manifestations and works of the enemy.

Jesus demonstrated how Adam should have functioned. He came to do the Father's will. Adam had been given the same authority and the same commission. In John 20:21b, Jesus said to His disciples, "... *as my Father hath sent Me, so send I you.*" As God had breathed into Adam the Spirit of Life, Jesus breathed on His disciples and said, "*Receive ye the Holy Ghost [or Holy Spirit]*" (John 20:23b). When we are "born again" we receive the life of the Spirit of God and we have the authority of that indwelling life.

Jesus prayed daily to the Father to discern His will. Adam and God communed daily in the cool of the day. The difference is that Jesus always chose the Father's will, even unto death. Adam chose to do his own will, disobeyed God and lost his life and his authority over the spirits. Therefore, all authority was given unto Jesus and He has delegated that authority to His disciples. After Jesus said to His disciples, "... *as My Father hath sent me, even so, send I you,*" and just before ascending to the Father, He told His disciples to go into all the world and preach the Gospel, heal the sick, cast out demons and make disciples, teaching others to do the same things that they had been taught. He did not say to stop, or to just do some of the things that they had been taught and not others. He said: "*Teaching them (nations) to observe **all** things, whatsoever I have commanded you and lo, I am with you alway, **even unto the end of the world**"* (Matt. 28:20).

The ministry of Jesus is an example to us of what to do and how to do it. In John 14:12, Jesus told his disciples:

Verily, verily, I say unto you, He that believeth on me, the works that I do shall he do also; and greater works than these shall he do; because I go unto my Father.

There are many scriptures to support the injunction to establish the Kingdom of God. We are to be overcomers and nothing shall be impossible to us. Jesus came to minister to the whole man: body, soul and spirit. He came that we might have life (chaiyim or zoe) and life more abundantly, as opposed to the thief who comes to steal, kill and destroy.

We are in a spiritual battle whether we care to admit it or not. Choosing to remain ignorant affords no protection from the scheming, destructive, diabolical plots of the enemy. We can learn how to fight and win or we can choose to sit in the dark and wait to be destroyed.

In a war, it is essential to understand the enemy. God has given us all the information that we need to defeat him and overcome him. We do not need to study the occult to know how to defeat Satan and his devices. The apostle Paul told us that we are not ignorant of Satan's devices. Studying counterfeit money does not teach us what we must know to detect counterfeit money. The only thing we need to know is what genuine money looks and feels like; then we will be able to spot the counterfeit. When we are thoroughly indoctrinated in the truth, we will be able to detect the lie. *"Ye shall know the truth and the truth shall make you free"* (John 8:32).

God gave man dominion over the works of his hands. To have authority on the earth, one must be born of woman; that is, of mankind. When we speak of "man" we are using the term to mean both male and female. God created man in His image and likeness. *Male and female created He them"* (Gen. 1:27b). God placed man on the earth for the purpose of governing it and enforcing the will of God. God did not give dominion to angels, animals or minerals. The will of man was to be the expression of the will of God. If Satan was going to get his will done, he would have to get it done through the will of man. God, having turned control over to man, had to work through man to get His will done. The battle between God and Satan comes down to the battle over the will of man. The prize of the battle is the will of man. God is looking for a man who will do His will. Satan is looking for a man who will do his will. Jesus said, *"... I seek not mine own will, but the will of the Father which hath sent me"* (John 5:38b).

The will of man determines his character. The decisions he makes and the action he takes will either further the Kingdom of God, or the kingdom of Satan. God wants us to serve Him willingly, of our own free will. Satan uses every device he can to get people to do his will, willingly or unwillingly. He will resort to lying, deception, or force to get someone to accomplish his nefarious schemes to kill, to steal and to destroy. When we are not doing God's will, we are doing Satan's. There is no middle ground. If you are not for God then you are against Him.

A slave is someone who does the master's bidding and has no choice but to obey him. In war, captives are made into slaves. They cannot escape and they must toil for their masters without recourse. Slave labor camps are found today in some parts of the world, and convicts and/or political prisoners are forced into these camps to work for the "state." Likewise Satan brings his prisoners into bondage and makes them do his bidding. Jesus came to set the captives free, to open the prison doors and let the captives go free. As the Father sent Jesus, so He sends us. *"To obey is better than sacrifice and to hearken than the fat of rams"* (I Sam. 15:22).

Man is a spirit, he has a soul and he lives in a body. To control man's body and to get him to do his will, Satan must control man's will. The will is part of the soul of man. The soul is the mind, the emotions and the will of man. There are two avenues to the will. One is through the mind and the other is through the emotions. Satan will try to control our actions by deceiving us concerning the truth. One of his most effective ways is to keep us ignorant of God's Word. If we do not know the truth, we will come into bondage. By keeping us in the dark, Satan is free to deceive us. One of Satan's greatest assets is an unrenewed mind that is full of "worldly wisdom." When we resort to thinking with reason and logic, devoid of the wisdom and knowledge of God, we will fail every time and wind up doing the will of the enemy. The Bible tells us that there is a way which seemeth right unto man, but the end thereof is DEATH.

If Satan can turn a truth into a lie, and make us believe that it is a truth, we will cleave to it, act upon it and it will bring forth death. II Corinthians 4:3-4 states:

But if our gospel be hid, it is hid to them that are lost:

In whom the god of this world hath blinded the minds of them which believe not, lest the light of the glorious gospel of Christ, who is the image of God, should shine unto them.

Without the knowledge of the Word of God, and left to our own reasoning, we will walk into the snares and pits of the enemy unawares. With false teachings, false doctrines and heresies, we will also be doing the will of Satan, thinking all the time that we are following God. We will be doing wrong things for the right reasons. Saul of Tarsus persecuted the church of Jesus Christ with great zeal, thinking that he was doing God a favor. When his eyes were opened to the truth, he spread the Gospel message with the same fervor and was himself persecuted. The specious reasoning of humanism is a particularly effective tool of Satan because it appeals to our sense of right and wrong. It puts special emphasis on fairness and situational ethics while excluding the concept of absolute truth and what is just and right according to God's Word.

To avoid the mind traps of Satan, we must have the mind of Christ. That is why Philippians 2:5-8 says:

Let this mind be in you, which was also in Christ Jesus:

Who, being in the form of God, thought it not robbery to be equal with God:

But made Himself of no reputation, and took upon Him the form of a servant, and was made in the likeness of men:

And being found in fashion as a man, He humbled himself, and became obedient unto death, even the death of the cross.

Jesus not only knew the will of His Father, but in every respect was totally submissive and obedient. How can we hope to have the mind of Christ? The answer is found in Romans 12:1-2: to present our bodies, a living sacrifice . . . and (v. 2) ". . . *be not conformed to this world: but be ye transformed by the renewing of your mind, that ye may prove what is that good, and acceptable, and perfect will of God.*"

The word "transformed" is translated from the Greek word meaning "metamorphosed". Any high school biology student knows that metamorphosis is the process by which a caterpillar is transformed into a butterfly. Our minds must undergo a metamorphosis to change our minds from Adamic and natural reasoning to the mind of Christ. We must remember that this is a process, and one which takes time. As we renew our mind by "eating" the words of God, we begin to know and understand the mind of God and take on His wisdom. Knowledge of the Word by itself tends to Pharisaism. I Corinthians 8:1 states, " . . . *Knowledge puffeth up but charity edifieth.*" It requires the Word of God and the Spirit of God to transform our minds into the mind of Christ. (Jesus had the Spirit without measure.)

Knowledge, without the Spirit, leads to pride, and pride is another ally of Satan. After all, it was the sin of pride that caused Satan to fall in the first place. Pride is the opposite of humility. Note the above passages carefully. In addition to keeping us ignorant of the Word of God (which is the expression of the will of God), Satan will attempt to infect us with demonic spirits which will effectively keep us from receiving the truth. I Timothy 4:1 says:

Now the Spirit speaketh expressly, that in the latter times some shall depart from the faith, giving heed to seducing spirits, and doctrines of devils (demons).

Once we have received a lie, it is almost impossible to receive the truth in that particular area. This is why certain denominational teachings which are contrary to the scriptures are difficult to dislodge from minds, even in the face of clear Biblical evidence. These teachings have blinded the person from the truth. A demonic spirit will control the person's thought processes and prevent the person from coming into conformity with the "image of God."

The other avenue to the will is through our emotions. Emotions, contrary to what many believe, are quite normal and appropriate. It is perfectly normal and healthy to experience and show emotion, even in church. Emotions were given to us by God. Without emotions, we would not be able to understand God. Adam was created in the image and likeness of God, and God has emotions. Any reading of the Bible will reveal the emotional nature of God. Even Jesus wept, rejoiced, grieved, had compassion and was angry. He experienced and felt rejection not only from man, but from God, His Father; when on the cross, Jesus cried out: *"My God, My God, Why hast thou forsaken Me?"* (Mark 15:34b).

All of these emotions are part of being human and being spirit. Trouble begins when we stifle our emotions, deny how we feel about something and fail to deal with it, usually out of fear or pride. Our reactions to situations reveal much about how mature and normal we are. If our emotions are normal, that is, normal by God's criteria, then we will react exactly as God would react emotionally in the same situation. God has emotions and He experiences emotions in His dealings with men. Jesus responded to every situation and person exactly as His Father would have.

It is not difficult to conclude that we do not often respond to circumstances and situations as Jesus did. Yet that is what God wants to accomplish in our lives. He says to bless them that curse you and to pray for them that despitefully use you. He says to turn the other cheek, and He says to go the extra mile. Some of these things we know to do, but our emotions block us from being obedient.

We are supposed to forgive. We are supposed to forgive the same person seventy times seven. Often we find it difficult to forgive the second time, much less the declared number. There are some who cannot forgive even the first time because of past hurts. People who know the truth and the importance of forgiveness but have a difficult time forgiving are usually in bondage. Again, Satan will try to get a foothold in us with a spirit of unforgiveness, or bitterness or hurts. Resentment, pride, envy, etc., keep us from doing God's will from a pure heart.

We talk about the infinite wisdom and the all-knowing mind of God, yet we think very little about the pre-eminent emotional attribute of God. The Bible tells us that God is love (agape). The quality of agape love is demonstrated in John 3:16: *"For God so loved the world that He gave His only begotten Son, that whosoever believeth on Him, shall not perish, but have everlasting life"* (zoe, not psuche). Jesus was the manifestation of that love and demonstrated that love in action every day of His life. He made Himself of no reputation, yet went about doing good and healing all that were oppressed of the Devil. When the time came, He willingly laid down His life that the world might be saved.

The quality of the love of God, the agape kind of love, is described in I Corinthians 13, the "Love Chapter," which describes the way we, as children of God, should be and feel. To the extent that we do not line up with the description found here, we are not in the image and likeness of God. When our chief emotion and motivation is agape love, our emotions will be comformed to the image and likeness of God's emotions.

Emotions are formed and developed in our earliest years. God's plan for the family is that children will be born into a family where there is love, security, protection, training and respect. A baby born into a family where he is loved, wanted and nurtured in the Word of God will grow up to be well balanced. The child learns how to love because he is loved. (We love God because He first loved us. You cannot give that which you never received!) Furthermore, a child who is accepted and affirmed by his father does not have an identity problem because of the secure feeling that he belongs and is supposed to "be." He will not suffer the low self-esteem suffered by a child who is not wanted.

In families where there is rejection, strife, envy, jealousy, anger, hate, dishonesty or a multitude of other negative factors, there will be disturbed problem children. Emotions that are damaged are easily infected, just as a body that has been badly cut and bruised, living in unclean surroundings, will get infected. An unwanted child will come into the world with a spirit of rejection and will never be secure or well-adjusted until that evil influence is removed from the emotions and enough positive, affirming and loving attention extended to heal and strengthen him.

The ministry of deliverance is a blessing to those who are infected with unclean spirits that keep them defeated and unable to be all that God called them to be. Without the authority that Jesus gave to His church, the power of the enemy to defeat us could never be broken. However, with that authority, we are more than conquerors. We have but to rise and conquer.

Since there are many books available which deal with the ministry of deliverance, we will not discuss it here.

What is germane to this work is that, like the physical world, infectious agents in the body produce recognizable symptoms. Indeed, most medical diagnosis is based on observation of outward symptoms. Even diagnosis with laboratory analysis, x-rays, sonograms or other diagnostic tools is predicated upon recognition of known patterns that indicate the presence of these agents.

The Bible says that even a child is known by his doings. So also are the spirits that attack and enslave us. The presence of specific spirits produces for the most part recognizable and predictable symptoms in their victim. A spirit of lust will manifest itself as lust. It may not always lust for the same thing in each person, but nevertheless it will produce lust of some sort. That is its nature. It cannot change its nature. A spirit of addiction will cause the victim to become addicted to something—maybe cigarettes or alchohol, or sugar, or food, or even prescription drugs. A lying spirit will cause a person to lie, even when there is no need or reason to lie.

Just as a medical doctor is trained to diagnose medical problems by trained observation, so the minister may learn to detect the presence of unseen spiritual forces by the manifestations of defeat or inappropriate behavior, or by emotional patterns in a person's Christian walk. One must be careful not to become preoccupied with demons or unclean spirits. Deliverance is a valid and vital ministry to the oppressed. But it is A ministry, not THE ministry. Believing that expelling demons will cure every problem is being naive, and not scriptural. Jesus only used it where there were demons. There were many circumstances where He laid hands on people and healed them. Other times He rebuked people, and at other times He taught them the truth and the truth made them free.

Getting rid of the spiritual infection in a victim is but one of the first steps to bringing the person to health and wholeness. A patient goes into the hospital and the first thing done is try to rid the body of infection and then treat other conditions. Performing an operation with infection in the body can be dangerous, and will be done only in an emergency or when the operation is necessary to eliminate infection attacking the body.

In the conflict between God and Satan, there are many casualties. Many people are wounded and have to be rescued, healed and rehabilitated. It is to that process that this book addresses itself. Treating battle wounds and eliminating infection is but the first step on the road to recovery. Following is the convalescence period, the therapy and the rehabilitation. It takes more than a wee bit of prayer. It requires time, energy, resources and ourselves poured out for the hurt and wounded. Jesus came to bind up the broken hearted, to set at liberty those that are bruised, and to let the captives go free. It is His ministry. He started it, He showed us how to do it and then He turned it over to us to continue.

The story of the Good Samaritan sets the stage for us. A man was bleeding and dying on the road to Jericho and the Samaritan stopped and ministered to him, pouring in the oil and the wine, but he did not stop there. Next, he took him to the inn on his own beast and then paid the innkeeper out of his own pocket to care for the poor man, promising to pay more if need be. Our responsibility does not end with rendering first aid. We must see the thing through. Even if it costs us! The Master has commanded it, so we should obey.

God has given us all things pertaining to life and godliness. There is nothing more that we need from Him. We have His Word, His Spirit and His promise, His power, His authority and His injunction. Arise, let us go hence.

Chapter 4

INIQUITY

And when Simon saw that through laying on of the apostles' hands the Holy Ghost was given, he offered them money,

Saying, Give me also this power, that on whomsoever I lay hands, he may receive the Holy Ghost.

But Peter said unto him, Thy money perish with thee, because thou hast thought that the gift of God may be purchased with money.

Thou hast neither part nor lot in this matter: for thy heart is not right in the sight of God.

Repent therefore of this thy wickedness, and pray God, if perhaps the thought of thine heart may be forgiven thee.

For I perceive that thou art in the gall of bitterness, and [in] the bond of iniquity. Acts 8:18-23.

The apostle Peter recognized that there were two roots to Simon's lust for power over people. These roots had been responsible for his involvement in the occult in the first place and, when he was converted, were not removed. The root of bitterness could easily come from rejection and is fairly widely understood. However, most Christians ask, "What is iniquity?", and you will probably be surprised at the answers, or lack of them. It is a phenomenon that a word that is so frequently used by God in speaking to His people is so poorly understood by the people to whom He speaks.

For many years, in my circle of Christian associates, there had been an unwritten and unspoken assumption that the Bible talked about "sin" and "iniquity" as if they were one and the same thing. I regarded them as being synonymous. They were, in my mind, virtually inter-changeable. Adding to this was the periodic reminder from Bible teachers, eager to display their academic knowledge of the oriental mentality, that the Jewish poetic style was to repeat each statement, rephrasing it for coloration and variety, giving emphasis by repetition. I submit that it is not repetition at all but God stating truth both in the spiritual realm and the physical realm. One statement relates to the natural, the other statement relates to the spiritual.

As an illustration, God told Abraham that his descendants would be as numerous as (1) the sands of the sea, and (2) as the stars of the heavens. This sounds very poetic, but one reference is clearly earthly, "sands of the sea," and the other heavenly or spiritual, "as the stars of the heavens." Abraham has innumerable descendants in the natural, both Jews and Arabs, and he has innumerable descendants in the spiritual realm through faith in Jesus Christ (Gal. 3:7, 29).

Not only did Abraham have many decendants through Isaac and Jacob, but also through Ishmael, his son by Hagar, and also the many other offspring through Keturah whom he married after the death of Sarah (Gen. 25:1). We see the many spiritual descendants of Abraham through the "Seed" of Abraham, that is, Christ, "... *not to seeds as of many; but as of one....*" We read in Hebrews 11:12:

> *Therefore sprang there even of one, and him as good as dead, so many as the stars of the sky in multitude, and as the sand which is by the sea shore innumerable*

Not having a foundation in either Hebrew or Greek, I assumed that "committing" sin was tantamount to "committing" iniquity. Whatever difference there was between the two words, it was not apparent to the casual Bible reader or Sunday morning student. My many teachers never made a point of delineating the difference between the two words. By looking carefully at each word and how it is used, it becomes clear that they are not synonyms at all. A simple study of the Hebrew words will reveal the differences between them.

When the Bible says sin, it is talking about transgressing the law of God. When the Bible talks about iniquity, God is talking about something else. While they are not the same, there is a causative relationship between the two. It is precisely this relationship that has caused the confusion in so many minds. Serious Bible students and certainly all Bible scholars must have known this all along, but the truth has never been exposed on a level that the average layman understands.

There has been precious little in the way of teaching on this most important subject. If Bible scholars and teachers truly understood the difference, I can only believe that there would be copious teachings on the subject. The absence of definitive teachings and exegetical works belies the dearth of true understanding of the nature of "iniquity."

In II Thessalonians 2:7, Paul spoke of the *"mystery of iniquity"* already working. I do not believe that he was referring to the lack of understanding of the word "iniquity" but to the mystery of how it works. There is that unseen and mysterious connection between a father's sins and the path of his children. If the father commits certain kinds of sin, his offspring are prone to the same kinds of sin, regardless of their training, or the social, cultural and environmental influences on them.

The Hebrew word for "sin" is "chatha" and the Hebrew word for "iniquity" is "avown." These words have very different meanings. A careful reading of selected scriptures reveals that sin is committed and iniquity is "passed down" to the children, to the third and fourth generation. It is not sin that is passed down, it is iniquity. Iniquity is not the transgression of the law, sin is. Transgressing the law is sin. When a person transgresses the law, iniquity is created in him and that iniquity is passed to his children. The offspring will be weak to temptation to the same kind of sin. Each generation adds to the cumulative iniquity, further weakening the resistance of the next generation to sin, as the apostle Paul stated in Romans 6:19:

> *I speak after the manner of men because of the infirmity of your flesh: for as ye have yielded your members servants to uncleanness and to iniquity unto iniquity; even so now yield your members servants to righteousness unto holiness.*

When the iniquity has intensified through several generations, there may be a compulsion to engage in certain kinds of sin, and more of the children will be adversely affected. Each generation is more wicked than the previous. The infamous family known as the "Terrible Williamsons" is a recent example. It is the principle of iniquity that desperately needs to be understood by every Christian and non-Christian alike as the unrestrained behavior of people, transgressing God's laws, will bring a nation to poverty and ruin.

(To be accurate, there are passages in the Bible referring to committing iniquity. If iniquity is a consequence of the commission of sin, then to commit sin is to also commit iniquity; however, you cannot commit iniquity independent of and apart from sin. Iniquity is a residual consequence of sin which affects not only the one sinning, but also the offspring of the sinner.)

Strong's Concordance defines "avown" or "avon" simply as perversity. The *Theological Wordbook of the Old Testament* states that "avon" is a derivative of the root word "awa" which means: to bend, twist, distort. Often, we do not see that which is plain because we are not expecting it and our minds do not comprehend what we are seeing. The Bible speaks on more than one occasion about having eyes but not seeing, having ears but not hearing.

What is it about iniquity that we have neither seen nor heard? Sin and iniquity are "spiritual" terms. We do not always grasp the significance of such terms as we would for something relating to the natural. Paul the apostle wrote plainly that the things not seen are understood by the things which are "made" (Rom. 1:20). He was referring to the natural universe, that is, creation, when he spoke of the things that are "made."

Drawing from the physical realm, we see that each species reproduces "after its own kind." Within every seed there is the inherent ability to reproduce itself. Even Jesus used this law of generation in the Sermon on the Mount when He said in Matthew 7:15-17:

> *Beware of false prophets which come to you in sheep's clothing, but inwardly they are ravening wolves.*
>
> *Ye shall know them by their fruits. Do men gather grapes of thorns, or figs of thistles?*
>
> *Even so, every good tree bringeth forth good fruit; but a corrupt tree bringeth forth evil fruit.*

This leads to the next question: "What causes bad or evil fruit?" In the natural, we know that if the fruit is malformed or the tree is not bearing fruit according to its stock, then a mutation has taken place. The same is true in breeding animals. If the offspring are not true to the breed, the breeders usually "eliminate" them from their pool of animals. Mutants are not wanted. They are a corruption of the line of animals being bred.

In the early 1940s, Adolf Hitler attempted to breed the "Master Race" through genetic selection of Aryans and the specific extermination of Jews from the biological pool. We should not find this strange since Satan tried to create his own species of people, destroying the stock of God's people and creating in their place his own wicked descendants.

In Genesis 6:4 we see that "... *the sons of God came into the daughters of men and they bare children to them,...*" These offspring are called "nephilim" in the Hebrew and the word is translated "giants" in the English. The exact meaning of the Hebrew word is uncertain. There are two possible root words in the Hebrew. The root may be from the word "palah," meaning "to separate," or from the word "naphal," meaning "to fall." There is support for the latter as they were the product of the "fallen angels" and the character of the offspring was more akin to them than to God, who created man.

In the first chapter of Genesis, God states the "law of generation." Everything reproduces after its own kind. (Every statement made by God in the opening verses of the Bible is a profound, powerful and fundamental truth. It is these very truths that are so under attack in the world today.) We acknowledge this principle in buying a pedigreed animal but we completely ignore this principle when we deal with people. Certain breeds of dogs are noted for their unpredictable and aggressive behavior and are not recommended to be around children.

It is interesting that God did not ignore this principle when He told the Children of Israel not to marry outside of the descendants of Jacob. Especially were they not to marry the Canaanites. Keep in mind that in the Old Testament there was no spiritual deliverance. Only when Jesus began His public ministry did the practice of casting out demons begin, and people could be set free from the bondage of unseen forces that drove and enslaved them.

When you go to a medical doctor for treatment of some organic disorder, he will usually take a "medical history" before he begins his diagnosis and treatment. What you tell him of your past problems, and the problems your parents, grandparents and siblings may have had, will have an effect on what he may look for or what tests he may order. Many diseases are genetic, that is, they are inherent in a family line and are inherited from one or both parents. These disorders may be in some or all of the offspring, or may occur in the grandchildren or great-grandchildren.

In such family disorders, there are specific encodings in the chromosomes that give rise to specific pathological conditions. Offspring get all of what they are from their natural parents: the color of hair, eyes, skin, body type, facial features, etc. These are all inherited characteristics and can only come from the biological parents. There is no decision on the part of the child as to what color the hair will be or anything else. There is no conscious decision on the part of the parents as to the sex, eventual height or temperament of the child. All these are a product of the gene pool carried by each of the parents. In Matthew 6:27, Jesus asked, *"Which of you by taking thought can add one cubit unto his stature?"* We are what we are from the moment of conception by the combinations of genes from our parents. No more, no less.

Healthy couples who have healthy ancestors almost always have healthy offspring. This is the law of generation. Because of the existence of genetic diseases that are potentially devastating, especially if there is inbreeding, there are prohibitions against near blood kin marrying. Diseases such as Tay-Sachs disease among Jews and sickle-cell anemia among Blacks are potentially disastrous if both parents carry the gene. Screening tests are recommended before marriage so decisions may be made whether to have children, or, indeed, whether to marry.

Now what does this have to do with iniquity? Everything! Genetic inheritance is a natural counterpart to spiritual inheritance. Understanding natural laws concerning genetic inheritance gives us a working model for the principle of spiritual inheritance. Mendel's laws describe the relationships and expected outcomes of matings of variants within a species. I believe that there is ample evidence to suggest that we may expect similar, if not identical, relationships to apply in the spiritual realm. The Bible gives examples of spiritual laws and their workings in the lives of various characters and their descendants.

The first example is Adam. Adam was created in the image and likeness of God. We will not go into all which that entails, but suffice it to say that something was significantly different about Adam after the fall. Genesis 5:3 states:

> *And Adam lived an hundred and thirty years, and begat a son in his own likeness, after his image; and called his name Seth:*
> *And the days of Adam after he had begotten Seth were eight hundred years: and he begat sons and daughters.*

Although the Bible never records another sin for Adam, one was enough to create a spiritual imperfection in at least one of his two sons. Cain rose up and slew Abel. (Note: We see in Genesis 4:23 that a descendant of Cain, Lamech, was also a murderer.) Cain had inherited the imperfection of the seed of the serpent and exhibited the traits of the one who was *"a murderer from the beginning."* It was not until after Seth was born that Eve prophesied that God had given her another "Seed," another son whose line could carry the righteous inheritance until the coming of the Messiah.

God told Eve that she would be saved in child-bearing. It was not the act of bearing children that would save her and mankind, but that, by her continuing to bear children, God would someday bring forth, through a woman, that Righteous Seed who would be the Savior of the world.

Without debating who the "sons of God" were in Genesis 6, or the true meaning of the nephilim, suffice it to say that Satan was attempting to defile and destroy the Seed of righteousness by polluting the women and establishing a line of descendants who were his progeny. In Matthew 8:44, Jesus declared the Pharisees to be vipers (serpents) and of their father, the Devil. Strong words, but Jesus knew their hearts and the iniquity within them.

With Satan trying to corrupt the entire human race to prevent God from bringing forth Messiah, the whole earth was overspread with evil and the thoughts of men were *"only evil continually."* All mankind had been perverted in their genealogy by sin, producing iniquity in the offspring. But Noah was perfect in his generation (genealogy). In other words, from Adam, through Seth, there was a line that had neither intermarried nor cohabitated with either the fallen angels or the sons of Cain; therefore, he was perfect, uncontaminated, in his "genes."

Even in this, there were some flaws in the genes of Noah and his sons; Ham especially was affected by the curse of iniquity. When Noah became drunk, he lost control of his son Ham, the weakness to sin caused him to give way to temptation, and the Bible says that Noah was "uncovered" in his tent. The Hebrew word that is translated into the English word "uncovered" is used in Leviticus many times, mostly in regard to proscribed sexual sins involving incest.

It is highly unlikely that it was a simple case of nudity. The curse that Noah pronounced on Canaan was too drastic for such a trivial thing as that. When we regard God's displeasure with homosexuality, we see this kind of judgment.

Further reading of the scriptures will confirm that this was indeed the case with Ham. In Genesis 15, we read that God gave assurance to Abram (Abraham) that he would inherit the Land of Promise because his descendants would go into a strange land for 400 years, but that after four generations they would return because " . . . *the iniquity of the Amorites is not yet full.*"

Now what does that mean and what does that have to do with Abraham inheriting the land? What is "full iniquity"? The Amorites were descendants of Canaan. They were in the land of Canaan. This is the land that the Children of Israel were to take by force from the Canaanites. These were the people who were worshiping all manner of idols and false gods and their worship was characterized by gross sexual perversions and orgies.

Recall also that in the thirteenth chapter of Genesis, when Abram and Lot had to separate, Lot chose the plain where the cities of Sodom and Gomorrah were located. The inhabitants of these cities were also Canaanites.

Their sin? Homosexuality! Abraham negotiated with God for the city so that if there would be ten righteous men found in the city, God would spare it. Only righteous Lot and his family were spared. The rest were totally corrupted. At that time, the iniquity of the Sodomites and the Gomorrahites was full.

By three or four generations of successive and cumulative iniquity, the children were so crooked and perverse that there was no possibility that they would ever walk "straight" or righteously. By four generations, their spiritual genes were completely corrupted. Their hearts were inclined to evil and they lived in a land full of evil. It was of the Canaanites that God said to Israel in Deuteronomy 20:16,17:

> But of the cities of these people, which the LORD thy God doth give thee [for] an inheritance, thou shalt save alive nothing that breatheth:
> But thou shalt utterly destroy them; namely, the Hittites, and the Amorites, the Canaanites, and the Perizzites, the Hivites, and the Jebusites; as the LORD thy God hath commanded thee:

The command was to kill everything that was alive and that breathed: people and animals. Kill everything that could harbor spirits. (New Testament evidence that animals can harbor spirits is that Jesus gave the spirits in the Gadarene demoniac permission to enter into the swine.) The iniquity and the spiritual infection of the Canaanites were so severe that they had to be eliminated from the land. To allow them to remain would subject Israel to severe danger of spiritual infection. As yet there was no "cure" for spiritual infection and it could have spread throughout all of Israel.

We find a parallel of this principle in the natural realm in the cattle business. If a single animal in a herd is found to have brucellosis, the entire herd is killed, burned and buried. The danger of not doing this is that the entire cattle industry is at risk. The disease is highly contagious and there is no cure. Not reacting to an infection could have disastrous effects. God told Israel to quickly eliminate those who committed certain kinds of sin. Sins unto death were such things as idolatry, witchcraft, adultery, sodomy, fornication, bestiality, blasphemy, murder and false prophecy, and cursing father or mother.

Israel got in serious trouble when they refused to execute God's judgments. They were to keep His commandments and to do His judgments. Neglecting to eliminate the guilty allowed iniquity to multiply and, when the land fell to iniquity, God would have to bring in the sword and purify the land. The ninth chapter of Ezekiel is a vivid picture of God having to cleanse the land. In chapter 8, we see the charge God had against Israel: idolatry with its attendant deterioration of morals and social disciplines. In chapter 9, the angels were sent through the city slaying everyone who did not have the "mark" of God on his forehead—the ones sighing for righteousness (Ezek. 9:5-7).

> *And to the others he said in mine hearing,*
> *Go ye after him through the city, and smite: let not your eye spare, neither have ye pity:*
> *Slay utterly old [and] young, both maids, and little children, and women: but come not near any man upon whom [is] the mark; and begin at my sanctuary. Then they began at the ancient men which [were] before the house.*
> *And he said unto them, Defile the house, and fill the courts with the slain: go ye forth. And they went forth, and slew in the city.*

The prophet recoiled in anguish at the slaughter and feared that none would be left of the Children of Israel. God's reply was to tell him that the thing that He was doing was indeed necessary (vv. 9, 10).

> *Then said he unto me, The iniquity of the house of*

Israel and Judah [is] exceeding great, and the land is full of blood, and the city full of perverseness: for they say, The LORD *hath forsaken the earth, and the* LORD *seeth not.*

And as for me also, mine eye shall not spare, neither will I have pity, [but] I will recompense their way upon their head.

God then assured the prophet that all would be well because in the end, after the judgments had fallen and the only ones left would be righteous, the generations that would come from them would be righteous and serve the Lord. God spoke assuringly (Ezek. 14:22-23):

Yet, behold, therein shall be left a remnant that shall be brought forth, [both] sons and daughters: behold, they shall come forth unto you, and ye shall see their way and their doings: and ye shall be comforted concerning the evil that I have brought upon Jerusalem, [even] concerning all that I have brought upon it.

And they shall comfort you, when ye see their ways and their doings: and ye shall know that I have not done without cause all that I have done in it, saith the LORD *God.*

Shortly after this prophecy, the Babylonians laid seige to the city of Jerusalem and took it with great slaughter, taking a small remnant off to Babylon. After seventy years of captivity, the remnant was returned to Jerusalem to rebuild first the Temple and then the city itself.

God sees the heart, and the iniquity that lurks there. In Isaiah 48:8, God declared rebellious Israel a *"transgressor from the womb."* Lamentations 5:7 states:

Our fathers have sinned, and are not; and we have borne their iniquities.

Iniquity, like sin, must be dealt with. Unconfessed sin is "still on the books." When God made a covenant with

Israel, He made provisions for sin and iniquity. For there to be a covering for sin, there had to be the shedding of blood. *"The soul that sinneth, it shall die."* The Mosaic covenant made provision for the reconciliation to God through the typical sacrificial offerings of animals.

In Leviticus 26, God again told Israel that for faithful obedience He would bless them and for continual disobedience He would bring judgment upon them, including scattering what was left of them among their enemies. In verse 39, God told them that they would *"pine away in their iniquities and in the iniquities of their fathers in the lands of their enemies."* Then in verse 40, God told them that if they would confess their iniquity and the iniquity of their father's house, with their trespass, and humble their hearts and accept their punishment, then He would remember the covenant (v. 45).

It was this promise that Daniel stood upon when, in the ninth chapter of Daniel, he prayed to God, confessing the sins, trespasses and iniquity of the people and their fathers (vv. 4-19). Immediately after that confession, the Medes overran the Babylonians and Cyrus, king of Persia, ordered the Temple at Jerusalem to be rebuilt and sacrifice to the God of Heaven be made on his behalf.

In Nehemiah 1:5-11, we see Nehemiah praying to God after hearing about the condition of Jerusalem and the remnant of the Jews left in the land. Nehemiah also remembered the promise of God in Leviticus 26:40. He confessed their trespass and their iniquity, and the iniquity of their fathers' house. Shortly after that, the king of Persia, who now held them captive, granted Nehemiah permission to return to Jerusalem to rebuild the city and the walls. The restoration process begun by Daniel's prayer, which resulted in the rebuilding of the Temple at Jerusalem, was continued by Nehemiah's prayer and the rebuilding of the city.

In this, we see the pattern for restoration. First, even in captivity and with the land desolate, humility, confession, acceptance of responsibility for past actions and the recognition of our sinful nature inherited from our forefathers will lead to reestablishment of worship. After we are truly worshiping God, continued submission, confession and obedience will bring the hand of God into our lives on our behalf.

Another example of the workings of iniquity is in the story of King David. The Bible says that David was perfect in all his ways except in the matter of Uriah the Hittite. David's adultery with Bathsheba resulted in her becoming pregnant. Since her husband, Uriah, was away at war, David had him recalled to Jerusalem immediately, hoping that when he arrived he would be eager to have conjugal relations with his wife; this being so close to the actual conception, the adultery would probably go unnoticed. By such a ruse David hoped to conceal his sin.

David's plan did not work because Uriah was a man of very high principles. He would not enjoy the company of his wife while his men were on the battlefield. David's plan "B" was to have Uriah killed in battle so he could never find out about the affair and openly accuse David and Bathsheba.

After Uriah's death in battle, David married Bathsheba, but God told Nathan the prophet to confront David concerning his sin. Upon being confronted, David confessed his sin and was ready to accept the judgment. God told David that he would not die for the sin, although, according to the law of Moses, he and Bathsheba should have been stoned to death. What God did say was that, because he had done this thing, mischief would arise out of his own household and that the sword would never depart from his house. The incestuous rape of Tamar by Amnon set the stage for the revengeful murder of Amnon by Absalom. Later Absalom stole the hearts of Israel and revolted against his father, David. David had to flee from Jerusalem for his life.

As he left the city ahead of Absalom's advance, a man of deposed king Saul's house came out and cursed David and threw rocks and dust on him, hurling insults against him.

David's general, Abishai, asked permission to kill him for his actions against the king, but David told him not to touch him, saying to Abishai, *"God told him to curse me this day"* (II Sam. 16:10). David knew that he was under the judgment and chastisement of God and as he said (v. 12), *"It may be that the LORD will look on mine afflictions, and that the LORD will requite me good for his cursing this day."*

Not only did David lose four of his sons, but the sword never departed from his house. David's problem was one woman. Solomon, David's son by Bathsheba, took to himself seven hundred wives and three hundred concubines. It was the wives of the heathen that turned his heart from following God. Solomon's iniquity, inherited from his father, was a weakness for women. This desire made him vulnerable to spiritual infection through the pagan women that he coveted. These women were from nations that worshipped false gods, and the Children of Israel were forbidden to marry them. When Solomon married them, the spirits of idolatry that infected the women were picked up by Solomon through sexual intercourse and in his later years he was up on the mountain worshiping those same gods!

There are other occasions in the Bible where spirits of idolatry were picked up through marriage. Ahab, king of Israel, son of Omri, ascended the throne of Israel and it is noted that *". . . he did evil in the sight of the LORD above all that were before him. And it came to pass, as if it had been a light thing for him to walk in the sins of Jeroboam the son of Nebat, that he took to wife Jezebel the daughter of Ethbaal king of the Zidonians, and went and served Baal, and worshipped him"* (I Kings 16:30-31). Furthermore, King Ahab built a house and an altar to Baal in Samaria and caused the people of Israel to worship Baal.

In II Kings 8:16-18, we read about king Jehoram *". . . walked in the way of the kings of Israel, as did the house of Ahab: for the daughter of Ahab was his wife: and he did evil in the sight of the LORD."*

Worshiping false gods is spiritual adultery. Those who engage in idolatry eventually drift into physical adultery and perversion. The Old Testament presents the historical evidence of this principle, and the apostle Paul stated it plainly in his letter to the church at Rome, in Romans 1:18-32. There is an old axiom that says, "What the fathers do in moderation, the children do in excess."

In Ezekiel 18, we see the proverb of the "sour grapes" explained. The allusion to fathers eating sour grapes and the children's teeth being set on edge is an allegory of the sins of the fathers directly influencing and affecting the nature, personality and proclivities of the child. One of the scriptures that speaks emphatically and eloquently to this is Isaiah 57:3-5:

> *But draw near hither, ye sons of the sorceress, the seed of the adulterer and the whore.*
>
> *Against whom do ye sport yourselves? against whom make ye a wide mouth, and draw out the tongue? [are] ye not children of transgression, a seed of falsehood,*
>
> *Enflaming yourselves with idols under every green tree, slaying the children in the valleys under the clifts of the rocks?*

We see God's dealing with other kings that were so wicked that God did not let their line continue. Specifically, there was Jereboam, king of Israel, who caused Israel to sin. It is recorded many times that he was responsible for many of Israel's problems. He was very wicked and led the Northern Kingdom into idolatry and started them toward apostasy.

Another king that we have already mentioned is Ahab. He too caused Israel to sin in worshiping Baal in addition to the sins of Jeroboam. Also Baasha, another king of Israel. All three of these were "cut off" and all of their male descendants were killed. God had to destroy their bloodlines because of their extreme iniquity.

We also see this in Matthew 23:28-32, when Jesus spoke to the Pharisees, saying:

> *Even so ye also outwardly appear righteous unto men, but within ye are* **full of hypocrisy and iniquity.**
> *Woe unto you, scribes and Pharisees, hypocrites! because you build the tombs of the prophets, and garnish the sepulchres of the righteous,*
> *And say, If we had been in the days of our fathers, we would not have been partakers with them in the blood of the prophets.*
> *Wherefore ye be witnesses unto yourselves, that* **ye are the children of them which killed the prophets.**
> *Fill ye up then the measure of your fathers.*

It was these men to whom He spoke who killed the greatest prophet of them all, even the Son of God, Jesus Christ. The iniquity of the fathers was at work in the Pharisees and they were too blinded to see it in themselves.

Under the Mosaic law, the priests and Levites were forbidden to marry anyone but the virgin daughters of the Levites or a widow of another priest. This was so much in evidence in the Word of God that genealogy was a fetish among the Pharisees of Jesus' day. The Pharisees were proud of their lineage and threw the circumstances of Jesus' birth in His face when He confronted them. They prided themselves both on their knowledge of the "Oral Law," and that their righteousness was assured by being the natural offspring of father Abraham. To prove the legitimacy of Jesus' claim to be the Messiah, Matthew opened his Gospel account with the complete genealogy of Jesus all the way back through King David to Abraham.

When you begin to comprehend the reality and power of iniquity, there are many passages in the Bible that become much more understandable, and you begin to see the wisdom of God. In Deuteronomy 7:2, God forbade the Children of Israel to intermarry with the Canaanites because *" . . . they will turn the hearts of your sons from following Me."* You might think only the average Israelite might be influenced by the pressure of a pagan wife and be moved to compromise in allowing her some latitude to practice her former religion and, through ignorance, get himself caught up in it. On the other hand we see that the power of the spirits of idolatry in these heathen women was strong enough to turn the heart of the wisest man (other than Jesus) to ever live. Solomon was not only wise, but he had knowledge of the Word of God, and God had appeared personally to him twice in his lifetime.

I Kings 11:2 says, *"Of the nations concerning which the LORD said unto the Children of Israel, Ye shall not go in to them, neither shall they come in unto you: for surely they will turn away your heart after their gods: Solomon clave unto these in love."* The word "clave" is the same word found in Genesis 2:24 concerning marriage: the man shall leave his father and mother and shall cleave to his wife, and the two shall become one flesh.

For this reason, Paul warned Christians about being unequally yoked. Believers should not marry unbelievers, but, under the New Covenant, when children are born to parents and only one of them believes the children are sanctified by the believing parent.

In the Old Testament, there was no deliverance from spiritual infection, and the power of iniquity drove the Children of Israel further and further away from God and faithfulness to the covenant. When Jesus began His public ministry He had authority over the unclean spirits and He cast them out of people. Jesus came to do more than to make it possible for our sins to be forgiven. God not only recognized the sin problem but also the heart attitude that made it so easy to fall into sin. This heart attitude was a consequence of iniquity. This attitude had to be changed for a person to want to follow God.

In Jeremiah 31:33-34, God declared to Israel that under the New Covenant He would put His laws *" . . . in their inward parts, and write it in their hearts; and . . . will forgive their iniquity and remember their sins no more."* Also in Isaiah 53, God declared that *"He* (Jesus) *was bruised for our iniquity...*" and... "*the Lord hath laid on Him the iniquity of us all.*"

In Titus 2:14 we are told that we are redeemed from our iniquity and purified unto Christ. Only in the New Covenant can we be loosed from the bondage of our iniquities in one generation and be made a "new man" in Christ. It is only the true Christian who can be regenerated to newness of life. A person who has been "born again" of the Spirit of God can claim a Father in whom there is no iniquity, and therefore can overcome the flesh and the sin nature of Adam. As I Peter 1:23 states:

Being born again, not of corruptible seed, but of incorruptible, by the word of God which liveth and abideth for ever.

We are born of the seed of Christ. Isaiah 53:10 tells us that "*... when thou shall make his soul an offering for sin, He shall see His seed.*" Our regenerated spirit is of the seed of Jesus Christ, without sin and without iniquity. He kept Himself spotless for our sakes. In John 17:19, Jesus prayed to His Father, saying:

And for their sakes I sanctify myself, that they also might be sanctified through the truth.

This principle is again confirmed in I John 3:9, which states:

Whosoever is born of God doth not commit sin; for His seed remaineth in him: and he cannot sin, because he is born of God.

It is important that fathers understand that their own sins will impact their children. It is not enough to tell your children what to do or not do. They are subject to the effects of the iniquity of the fathers. They will be vulnerable to the same kinds of sin in which the fathers indulged. Fathers must sanctify themselves for the sake of their children. This is not to say that it does not matter what the mother does or does not do. The teaching and influence of the mother is very real, and can have a great effect on the behavior and attitude of the child, but the Bible states that the iniquity of the father is passed to the third and fourth generation.

In Matthew 7:24-27, the conclusion of the Sermon on the Mount sums up the principle very articulately. Jesus said that a man who hears the words of Christ and does them is like a man who builds his house on a foundation of rock. When the storms come, the house will stand. But a man who hears the words of Christ and does not do them is like the man who builds his house on sand. When the storms come, the fall of his house is very great.

The full force of this parable will come when you equate the word "house" to "family." All through the Bible, "house" is repeatedly used as a synonym for family or descendants. We understand that the "house of David" means the family descended from David. The "house of Saul" means the descendants of Saul. A man who hears and does the words that Jesus speaks will build his family on the rock of Jesus Christ, and the temptations and trials that come against that house will not cause it to fall!

Being set free from the law written on stone does not free us from the law that is now written on our heart by the Holy Spirit. To truly break the bondage of sin and iniquity over ourselves and our children we must be born again of that incorruptible seed, repent of our sins, confess the iniquities of our fathers and walk in the Spirit. As we continue in obedience to God, we sanctify ourselves and build a spiritual inheritance for our children. Deuteronomy 6:30 promises us that if we continue to obey God with our whole hearts, He will circumcise our hearts and the hearts of our children.

The adverse and destructive effects of iniquity have been stressed in the preceding paragraphs for the purpose of exposing the long-term effects of iniquity in a family, and, ultimately, a nation. What are the long-term benefits of avoiding iniquity for our children? It is simple to say that the children will be blessed and not cause us trouble, but it is far more than that. We are still born under the curse of Adam and are sinners by nature until we meet Jesus and have the power of the Holy Spirit dwelling within us to transform us into a new creation.

Secular teaching would have us believe that children who turn out bad are the result of bad environment and training. What about Moses? Moses was adopted by Pharaoh's daughter when he was only two months old. He was taken into the palace and raised as Pharaoh's daughter's son. The Bible tells us that he was trained in all the wisdom of the Egyptians. The Egyptians worshipped all manner of false gods and their morals were hardly Victorian. As a young man, Moses could have had anything his heart desired. Who would have dared to say nay? Wine, women and song would have been his on a whim, but we are told that he decided to forego the pleasures of sin. It was his free-will decision. How could he be so intuitively strong when his environment and culture said it was all right to do such things ? The Egyptian code of ethics and conduct did not define morality in the same way as did Jehovah.

The answer lies in the fact that Moses' father was a Levite, that his mother was a Levite and that his fore-father, Levi, had a covenant with God, as did another forefather, Abraham. Even adoption and training did not change what Moses was in his spirit. The Bible says he was a proper child. Another example of the rewards of righteousness is found in the story of Joseph. Again, we see Joseph, subjected to rejection and deprivation, forced into circumstances not of his choosing, yet being faithful to God's commandments out of his own heart. His father, Jacob, had been a usurper, a cheat, and, after his transfor-mation, God changed his name to Israel.

Most people today have seen or heard of a family that adopted a child, and trained him in a good home, often with strong Christian principles. Yet the child grew up and became involved in drugs, sex or crime, thus breaking the hearts of the parents. Again, we ask why? Environ-ment and training are not everything. The iniquity of the fathers is as real as the color of a child's hair or eyes. The spiritual inheritance is not changed by the adoption process any more than is the genetic inheritance. Inherited diseases must be dealt with; so must inherited wickedness. Like it or not, we are responsible for our children. Under the New Covenant, we can break out of the bondage of the iniquity of our fathers, set our children free and then live so as to give them good spiritual genes by keeping good spiritual hygiene.

The scriptures illustrate the importance of avoiding iniquity in the first place rather than trying to deal with it after it has been created and passed down with increasing destructiveness. In Jeremiah 35, there is the fascinating story of the Rechabites. These Midianite nomads, living in the land of Israel at the time of the Babylonian invasion (about 607 B.C.), had been forced to take refuge in the city of Jerusalem against the invading armies of Nebuchadnezzar. They descended through Jonadab, son of Rechab, mentioned in II Kings 10. Jonadab helped Jehu destroy Baal worship in Israel after the death of Ahab and Jezebel.

The Rechabites were used by God as a testimony against Judah because, while Judah was disobedient to God's words, they were obedient to Rechab's commandment not to drink wine or live in houses or plant fields, etc., for over 250 years. To prove that they were faithful to the command of their natural fathers, God told the prophet Jeremiah to have the Rechabites to come to a sumptuous room and with wine before them they would be invited to drink. They refused, in spite of the obvious social pressure to partake.

In Jeremiah 35:2ff God said to the prophet:

> *Go unto the house of the Rechabites, and speak unto them, and bring them into the house of the LORD, into one of the chambers, and give them wine to drink.*
>
> *Then I took Jaazaniah the son of Jeremiah, the son*

of Habaziniah, and his brethren, and all his sons, and the whole house of the Rechabites;

*And I brought them into the house of the L*ORD*, into the chamber of the sons of Hanan, the son of Igdaliah, a man of God, which [was] by the chamber of the princes, which [was] above the chamber of Maaseiah the son of Shallum, the keeper of the door:*

And I set before the sons of the house of the Rechabites pots full of wine, and cups, and I said unto them, Drink ye wine.

But they said, We will drink no wine: for Jonadab the son of Rechab our father commanded us, saying, Ye shall drink no wine, [neither ye], nor your sons for ever:

Neither shall ye build house, nor sow seed, nor plant vineyard, nor have [any]: but all your days ye shall dwell in tents; that ye may live many days in the land where ye [be] strangers.

Thus have we obeyed the voice of Jonadab the son of Rechab our father in all that he hath charged us, to drink no wine all our days, we, our wives, our sons, nor our daughters;

Nor to build houses for us to dwell in: neither have we vineyard, nor field, nor seed:

But we have dwelt in tents, and have obeyed, and done according to all that Jonadab our father commanded us.

The simple obedience of the Rechabites contrasted sharply with the rebellious attitude and actions of the tribe of Judah, and God chided them severely for their persistent disobedience. In verses 16 and 17, God pronounced judgment against Judah because He had found a people who could obey even their natural father while Judah would not obey the voice of God.

> *Because the sons of Jonadab the son of Rechab*
> *have performed the commandment of their father,*
> *which he commanded them; but this people hath not*
> *hearkened unto me:*
> *Therefore thus saith the* Lord *God of hosts, the God*
> *of Israel; Behold, I will bring upon Judah and upon all*
> *the inhabitants of Jerusalem all the evil that I have*
> *pronounced against them: because I have spoken*
> *unto them, but they have not heard; and I have called*
> *unto them, but they have not answered.*

After pronouncing judgment on the house of Judah, God spoke to the prophet to tell the Rechabites (v. 19):

> *Therefore thus saith the* Lord *of hosts, the God of*
> *Israel; Jonadab the son of Rechab shall not want a*
> *man to stand before me for ever.*

It is recorded in *Smith's Bible Dictionary* that there is a tribe of Arabs, the Beni-Khabir, dwelling near the city of Mecca, who claim that they are the descendants of Jonadab, the son of Rechab. They are still holding to the old rules and are a testimony to the blessing of the promise that they would never lack a man to stand before Jehovah!

It should be noted that the command was not just to refrain from wine, but there were several other prohibitions which not only the men, but the women also, observed. The fact was that there was a general and universal observance of the commandment; the children of the next generation also observed the tradition and commandment of the fathers. The lack of rebellion is indeed remarkable. Children who obey their parents are prone to have children who obey them.

A modern example of this principle of the Rechabites is found in the United States in the Amish families of southern Pennsylvania. The traditions and lifestyles of the Amish continue generation after generation, with few opting for the modern "conveniences" and lifestyles of the 20th century. Even to this day, they do not have telephones, electricity, automobiles, radios, televisions or any of the trappings of modern America. They continue to obey the commandments of their fathers to have none of these. They still farm and live as they have for hundreds of years.

There must be a postscript to this chapter that addresses a very serious area. What about the woman? Where does she fit into this picture, especially in the families where the husband and father is clearly rebellious and has a history of sin and iniquity? There are many mothers who have borne children of reprobate husbands and fathers. How can their children be set free from the bondage of the iniquity of their father? Because of the work of the Cross, we have a better covenant! Under the New Covenant, the children are sanctified by the believing parent (I Cor. 7:14). If the mother is a believer, the children are sanctified by her. The mother must sanctify herself and stand against the enemy, who will attempt to claim the children through the iniquity of their father. The battle for these children may be intense, but many children are walking with the Lord today because of a godly, praying mother or grandmother. How much more are children blessed and protected by godly Christian parents!

An example of the blessings of godly mothers is found in II Timothy 1:5, where the apostle Paul, writing to young Timothy, reminded him:

> *When I call to remembrance the unfeigned faith that is in thee, which dwelt first in thy grandmother Lois, and thy mother Eunice; and I am persuaded that in thee also.*

Amazing Grace!

Chapter 5

REJECTION

If there is one problem to be singularly credited with the retardation of the body of Christ and the crippling of the saints, it must be REJECTION, with its resulting emotional damage. Most of the frustrating problems that a leader must deal with today usually have rejection, or the fear of it, as the root! Many churches, ministries or other groups that have been brought to ineffectiveness by internal strife and contention have been able to pinpoint the primary cause of that failure as problems arising out of the roots of rejection and insecurity.

Even leaders often battle with fears stemming from the damage of rejection, or from unforgiveness which has resulted from being rejected by those closest to them. Proverbs 18:14 states, *"The spirit of a man will sustain his infirmity; but a wounded spirit who can bear?"* The wounds of rejection, infected by unforgiveness and bitterness, open man up to spiritual tormentors and bondages which bring defeat. No other weapons in Satan's arsenal do as much ongoing damage to people, at all levels of spiritual maturity, as do the spirits of rejection and fear of rejection. These two spirits seem to team up and open doors for more oppression, deeper personality problems and more serious emotional difficulties than any others.

The damage of rejection undoubtedly accounts for the greatest area of need for healing in the body of Christ today. Yet, it is awkward to deal with in a book such as this since it is not necessarily a personality type in itself. However, it is common to virtually all the personality problems we will discuss. In some cases, rejection may be a root cause to a personality problem, and in other cases may be a secondary cause resulting from a deeper problem. The study of rejection is further complicated in that everyone has encountered it at some point, to some degree of intensity, and with some degree of residual effect on his personality. People usually carry the effects around with them like last year's garbage.

This chapter will not deal with the multitudes of causes for rejection, but rather its effect on attitudes and behaviors as displayed by individuals in the body of Christ. The following brief examples will illustrate situations that can exist in a group, as well as behavior that can be expected in individuals with a rejection problem. Further, we will attempt to describe how rejection may affect elements of the group, including the leader.

Have you ever considered that rejection caused the first murder? When God rejected Cain's sacrifice, the jealousy and feelings of inferiority that resulted did not lead to repentance, but to the murder of his brother. How many of you have felt the murderous attack of someone in the body, or of someone close, because they themselves were rejected when offering what they felt would be a new and better solution to a problem?

Rejection of Potiphar's wife by Joseph led to his being falsely accused and incarcerated for a crime he never committed. How often have you felt incarcerated and stifled by members of the body, or by someone near and dear to you? Although you may realize that their reaction to you is in response to their own experience of rejection, the rejection that you experience is painful nevertheless.

Public rejection of Moses' wife by Miriam and Aaron seeded the camp for rebellion and loss of confidence in the leader. This led immediately to leprosy and separation from the camp of Israel for Miriam. How often have you seen separation occur in the life of one who is prone to unjust criticism, and even rejection of leaders, which leads to rebellion? This is Satan's way of keeping the problems centered around the feelings of rejection now rapidly spreading through the body.

When people suffer from rejection and fear of rejection, they often become highly critical of their peers, as well as their leaders. Rejection causes people to compensate for their own low self-esteem and feelings of inferiority by tearing others down to the level on which they believe themselves to function. Have you ever felt the sting of criticism from your peers when you KNEW that they were being completely unfair? An ongoing effect of rejection is to either retard progress, or to paralyze it entirely. It operates this way: The rejected person becomes so apprehensive and fearful of rejection that he will no longer risk presentation of his ideas or opinions.

Rejection of Aaron's leadership by three men who felt slighted by God caused such a revolt that 250 died in one day. The problem did not stop at this point. The next day the people attacked Moses because of God's intervention, accusing Moses of being totally responsible for the death of the 250. Thousands more died as a result of this new attack on Moses' leadership. Israel never again rested under Moses' leadership, causing repeated and serious spiritual missteps. Have you ever watched someone go on the attack to cover his own bitterness with God for rejecting what he believed was his call to leadership? Have you ever watched someone at work who would even destroy another's reputation to gain approval and acceptance for himself? Before we respond with too much anger for this behavior, we should take into consideration the effects of repeated rejection.

As believers we love to quote, teach and receive great comfort from the fact that Jesus experienced and was touched by everything that touches us. The problem is that just as Hebrews 4:14-15 gives us great solace, it is also the greatest catalyst for change, deliverance and maturity. This in turn SHOULD force us to forgive and to release last year's garbage. Who can remain behind the barriers caused by rejection when these verses have become LIFE to us?

> *Seeing then that we have a great high priest, that is passed into the heavens, Jesus the Son of God, let us hold fast our profession.*
> *For we have not an high priest which cannot be touched with the feeling of our infirmities; but was in all points tempted like as we are, yet without sin.*

Hurt and rejection were commonplace for Jesus. How many times do we find recorded events that clearly point out the rejection He suffered? Not only did the religious leaders of His day reject Him, but also those who found His message too hard, and His standards too costly. Even as He prepared for His death, He was trying to explain to the disciples that the Messiah had to go to Jerusalem and suffer the ultimate rejection, not only by the Scribes, Pharisees and the multitudes, but also by one of His own group. Judas had eaten with Him, walked with Him, shared in His victorious moments, even dreamed of establishing the Kingdom of God on this earth! Most of us can understand the pain of having someone close to us turn and try to destroy us after we shared so much of life. But do we totally understand the healing which Jesus poured out that day to free us from the effects of rejection? The power of that work leaves us with the ability to care again, to reach out again and to trust again!

If we begin to understand the power of this part of Jesus' ministry, then Isaiah 53:3-5 will take on new meaning in our lives, in our relationships and in the manner in which we minister and receive ministry. Verse 3 of this passage will become a cornerstone of our development because He pressed forward, in spite of it all, and fulfilled verses 4-12 of the same chapter.

But in all this, even identifying with the nature and hurt Jesus suffered, we imagine that our Heavenly Father remains unaffected, unharmed, untouched, unmoved and still distant from the stinging pain of rejection.

Sometimes we are guilty of believing that the Father is stoic in nature, devoid of understanding and compassion for those painful bruises that Satan and sin have brought into this world. We perceive our Heavenly Father as one holding out a standard so rigid that except for the life of Jesus we would all fall short, anticipating only punishment and separation.

This could not be further from the truth! Our Heavenly Father knows WELL the sting of rejection, since He was the first to receive it, in heaven and on the earth! In both Isaiah 14 and Ezekiel 28 we find recorded the first occurrence of rejection. Consider this scenario and how the Father must have felt. Heaven was running along perfectly. All was exactly as He created it to be and He was perfectly content. The music and worship were beautiful beyond description. Each angel was performing his assigned chores without complaint, even joyously. Then the Bible says that iniquity was found in one of the special created beings, one who knew Him best, the archangel who spent more time in fellowship with Him because he was in charge of music and led the heavenly worship. Lucifer's response to the iniquity found in him was not heart repentance. Instead he led a revolt, rejecting the Father's rule over the perfect beings He created.

Can you imagine the pain of the Creator being told by the creation that He was deficient, and no longer equipped to lead His own creation? Can you imagine the pain of war and of His loss, when the Father had to separate Himself for eternity from those He had created in love, and in desire for communion? Most of us would have become discontent, mistrusting, suspicious of everyone and totally unwilling EVER to take another risk. We would be sure that something was terribly wrong with US. If we ever dared try again, we would "hedge our bets" and make sure that NOTHING could happen to hurt us like that again. But not our Father, PRAISE HIS NAME! Not only did he try again, He even made man a little lower than the angels who revolted the first time.

The Father did try again, and in Genesis chapters 1-3 is recorded God's second, and possibly more painful encounter, with rejection! In Genesis chapter 1, verse 26, we read:

And God said, Let us make man in our image, after our likeness: and let them have dominion over the fish of the sea, and over the fowl of the air, and over the cattle, and over all the earth, and over every creeping thing that creepeth upon the earth.

From this, we realize that man was made in the image of God, had control over his environment, and lacked no good thing. Peace and harmony ruled.

In verse 8 of Genesis chapter 2 we get a still deeper picture of how good God was to man, how special God felt man was, and to what lengths God went for man's happiness:

And the Lord God planted a garden eastward in Eden; and there he put the man whom he had formed.

An extra benefit to Garden Living is found in Genesis 3:8:

And they heard the voice of the Lord God walking in the garden in the cool of the day....

How exciting it must have been to walk with the Father in the cool of every day. All went well for a season, and then Satan slipped into the Garden and convinced man that his way was better than God's way. Because God was totally good and could not teach man about evil, man would always lack what we would now call a well-rounded and sophisticated education. Unfortunately, man agreed with God's enemy and ate of the one forbidden tree in the garden. Once again, the Father's government of love and care was overthrown. Once again the beauty of God's creation was marred by that creation's rejection of its creator—of His ways, and His benefits!

Can we ever understand the level of pain in the heart of

the Godhead that day? Yet His response was one of forgiveness and reconciliation. He immediately opened a NEW WAY into His presence!

How many times have we felt the sting of rejection from someone whom we have just helped to have a better or more productive life in God, or a happier marriage, or a more fulfilled life professionally? As a result, how many of us have separated ourselves from everyone and everything, with our walls put up so high that NO ONE could get close again? But as we finish reading this Biblical account, the Father's love and purity shine forth to direct us to His healing. This healing has been made available for us through the life of the Son, and ministered through the power of the Spirit, as we apply the lesson He finished for us. You see, He immediately prepared a sin offering and taught reconciliation to His creation through the power of forgiveness!

In Exodus 19, we find God again desiring direct rulership and communion with His people. So He instructed Moses to tell the people to get ready, because in three days He would come down and speak with them so they would believe and remain steadfast.

How grateful, how full of love and thanksgiving toward the Father we would expect His people to be! The Father had just ended 400 years of slavery for them, and in the process had broken the back of every demon god that had harassed or tormented them, or that had attempted to kill all the spiritual life and hope they had left. He had brought them out at high noon the obvious victors, with treasures being thrown at their feet to repay them for all the years of toil, shame, abuse and death.

When we pick the story up in chapter 20, verses 18-19, we discover that:

> . . . *all the people saw the thunderings, and the lightnings, and the noise of the trumpet, and the mountain smoking: and when the people saw it, they removed, and stood afar off.*

> *And they said unto Moses, Speak thou with us, and we will hear: but let not God speak with us, lest we die.*

How sad and hurt the Father must have been! The people all saw the splendor around HIS HOLINESS. But instead of rejoicing that such a righteous God cared for them, they attributed to Him the character of the demon gods from whom they had been freed. How often are we rejected by people who cannot separate us from every evil or hurtful situation they have encountered? How often have we felt misunderstood, and by the very people who should know and trust us most? But more important, how often have we mistrusted those we should have been the safest with, even the Father Himself?

Once again our Father was rejected at a time of vulnerability, as He expressed His love and His desire for fellowship. How often do we feel misunderstood when we attempt to reach out, when we leaders misunderstand God's reaching out to us, to develop us or an aspect of our ministry?

We pick up the narrative in Exodus 20:21:

> *And the people stood afar off, and Moses drew near unto the thick darkness where God was.*

We must understand that life, healing, direction, purpose and identity are found in the Presence of God, even though the Presence of God, at times, takes us through the darkness of painful experiences. We must learn that God often allows us to learn mercy and compassion at the hands of people who are themselves so wounded that they can allow no one else peace, lest there be a negative reflection on their own turmoil.

The only thing gained by the people, for all their avoidance of the darkness where God was, was a second-hand relationship with the Father, one in which everything was colored by Moses' views and reactions. No matter how "on fire" for God, or even spiritually superior, someone else is, if we allow our own relationship with God to come through another, then we receive less than what God intended. Thus our walking out of God's plans and purposes becomes much more complicated, and committing sin much easier. Further, we allow the hurts we receive at the hands of others to keep us in a rejected state. It then becomes easier to accept a second-hand relationship with the Father in order to avoid His dealing with our hurt and wounded spirits. By such failure to really know Him, and to know His character, what fellowship we miss (I John 1:3). How much power and authority we sacrifice.

If we, as people who minister God's life and love, can learn from these situations, we will be able to identify those who have been badly rejected or abused, since they will always attribute the behavior of the abuser to us. They will always keep their distance from us and try to put as many people as possible between us in relationships. They will often appear completely uncooperative and aloof, in spite of our best efforts to draw them closer.

Do not take personally these behavior patterns, but understand that rejection is one of the reasons for such behavior. Begin to minister God's acceptance and unquestioning life and freedom to them.

In I Samuel 8:1-22, we find the next recorded rejection of the Father. Here the Children of Israel demanded a king for two reasons:

1. So they could never again be hurt and rejected by what they believed to be poor caretakers of God's plans and God's directions. (Samuel's sons did not live the life of purity and dedication that their father did.)

2. They no longer wanted to be rejected by the world around them because they looked so different and never seemed to fit in. After all, their leader was invisible. Even after Samuel tried to warn them of the problems they would face, they said, in effect, "We do not care, we must put another layer of distance between us and God!"

How often have we ourselves felt the knife of rejection cut deep, as a group of friends or family appointed a new leader, or formed a new friendship because they believed they would be better served? To our minds no understanding comes, because often we are guilty of caring too much, trying too hard to get close to them, and helping them be victorious over the spiritual enemies in their lives.

If Samuel's hurt was deep, and we can draw that conclusion from God's response to him, imagine how deep the hurt must have been for the Father. So often we say to the Father, "I have a better way, God. I cannot trust You to lead me without undue pain and loss." Or we say, "God, I cannot walk Your way. I'm tired of being laughed at. Your laws make me seem so different."

We must deal with the reactions of rejected people in the same manner as does our Father, with patience and long-suffering. Then, as we minister the balm of healing, as the Father did, we will see more and more healed people restored to the Kingdom. For the Father constantly said to all those who rejected Him:

1. I still love you.
2. I have not changed My mind about your potential or your place in My heart.
3. I choose to apply forgiveness.
4. I still call you My people.
5. I will not change My mind about your future with Me.

If we could learn not to give up but always to walk in the healing and forgiveness we ourselves have received, Satan's biggest attack on the body of Christ would completely fail. And if we, like the Father, could understand the problems suffered by the one rejecting us, perhaps we could respond with compassion. Therefore it would be great wisdom, when dealing with someone reacting adversely because of rejection, to pray and ask for the Holy Spirit to reveal his point of need and hurt.

Surely, as we realize that the Father Himself was regularly rejected, it will become easier for us to enter His Presence and to admit our need for His healing touch. We know that not only does He understand the cause of pain in our lives, but He also has been touched by the same wound. Therefore His touch in our lives will be gentle, and full of love and understanding for our pain and confusion.

As we encounter troubled people and are led by the Father to minister to them, the following may be a helpful list of characteristics, symptomatic behavior patterns, or verbal expressions that will reveal those suffering from rejection.

1. They tend never to regularly exercise their God-given talents and abilities.

   a. They may occasionally share a word or song with the body but never on a regular basis.

   b. They will usually refrain from using any gift that will reveal anything about themselves.

   c. They will often express jealous feelings about others who do use their gifts.

   d. They frequently require the leader to almost force them to share their talent. When that attention is not forthcoming, hurt is the result, often expressed by attack.

2. They will usually both openly and indirectly attack the leader or the person by whom they are most threatened.

3. Due to their past experiences with rejection, they will often attack first when they fear that someone is about to reject them.

4. Rejected individuals have such a strong survival instinct that they will attack the character or reputation of others because of their own needs for acceptance.

5. They will reject others first before others have an opportunity to reject them. They have such a low level of self-esteem that they expect rejection.

6. Individuals suffering from rejection share certain traits with victims. They know how to push you until you reject them, just as they told themselves and everyone else that you would. We understand that

it was the farthest thing from your mind at the time. (Some even have an ability to maneuver you into a position where your rejection of them occurs publicly.)

7. Rejection adds to their need to draw into a shell. They often give the impression that their entire lives are lived in their heads. You are never quite sure of their feelings, thoughts or reactions. Often you feel as though you are reaching out to them only to hit a barrier of some type.

8. If the people suffering from the effects of rejection also have tendencies toward the victim personality, not only will they withdraw but they will fight a terrible battle with doubt and unbelief. (They will have a very difficult time trusting you, but an even more difficult time trusting God. They will attribute to Him personality traits and motives that spell only hardship and pain for themselves, and great good for others.)

9. Rejection causes its captives to be extremely and irrationally fearful. If they already suffer from fearful or phobic personalities, then the initial work becomes extremely complex. There must be a trust level established not only with you, but also with God. These people are so very fragile that even slightly threatening, overpowering or future-oriented statements can bring a momentary freeze to progress.

10. The very nature of rejection causes loneliness which pushes its captives deeper into other personality problems.

11. Low self-esteem is always present because the fear of rejection forces them to negatively evaluate themselves.

12. The effect of rejection produces a strong sense of non-being, or "I am not."

13. A result of the preceding three traits is people who not only fight an ongoing battle with rejection, but

who are also internally preoccupied. This in turn causes them to find ministering to the needs of others almost impossible, because their own needs tend to overwhelm their emotional reserves.

14. It seems that every person suffering from the effects of rejection feels totally unworthy of any good thing, any recognition for accomplishment or any compliment regarding his personality or personal appearance.

15. The aforementioned trait complicates their spiritual life more than any other, because it creates the next attitude, which is an inability to accept their own salvation. This causes the following reactions, thus resulting in strain and strife in both churches and para-church groups.

a. They constantly set up standards that are too high to be met by anyone.

b. They are so critical of themselves and their spiritual life that they never seem to bear fruit.

c. They judge everyone by their own standards, and therefore find no one good enough to serve.

d. They can never receive forgiveness for their own lives.

e. They find forgiving and letting go of animosity toward others impossible.

f. They constantly remind others of their own weaknesses and repeatedly need counseling for the same problems.

g. They gain a reputation for self-pity.

h. They remember everyone else's shortcomings and sins and slyly bring them up when the "need to destroy someone" arises.

16. Since they cannot accept their own right to receive salvation, they become performance-oriented and controlled. This causes them to demand high levels of performance from everyone, including themselves. If they also suffer from an addictive or compulsive personality, you may think them a runaway train

completely out of control, or even a perpetual-motion machine that NO ONE can keep up with. This makes those who are ministering to them believe they are only as good as their next effort; also that they can never breathe easy or assume that a level of trust has been established in the relationship.

17. After a period of sustained difficulty with rejection, these people add a self-righteous attitude to their defense mechanisms.

18. As they continue, they become so distrusting of people and of God that they demand to be in control of their lives at all times!

19. They then progress to thinking of God as a harsh, demanding authority figure who requires behavior impossible to produce. Sometimes they also believe Him to be a harsh and unreasonable disciplinarian. They honestly do not understand anyone who sees God in any other way.

20. They tend to fight regular and serious battles with:

    a. Self-pity.

    b. Depression.

    c. Moodiness that can best be described as severe mood swings for no valid reasons.

    d. An internal striving and restlessness.

    e. Selfishness, and a demand for constant emotional support.

    f. Critical and judgmental spirits.

    g. Sometimes a real tendency to SHOW OFF.

21. These emotional swings force them to create false images in order to survive.

22. They tend to be crowd pleasers, which makes them more frustrated and resentful than ever.

When dealing with rejected people you must get them to understand the truth that Jesus taught in John 17, that He is in us, and that the Father is in Him, and that therefore God is His Father and ours as well. They MUST learn that they are accepted in the beloved Christ. This fact cannot be mere mental knowledge; it must be heart knowledge and understanding. They must come to realize, believe, and accept as fact that the living GOD who knows all there is to know about them loves them unequivocally. Once they can receive and believe that they are truly loved and accepted, they will be open to receive the healing they need. As you can see, deliverance is just the beginning. It must be ministered with much healing, with much love, and followed with much self-discipline. Rejection is usually tied to other personality problems, and the spirits associated with those problems must be dealt with accordingly.

The following brief list of spirits typically found with rejection may give some added direction.

A. Rejection.
B. Fear of rejection.
C. Self-righteous.
D. Criticism.
E. Strife.
F. Contention.
G. Judgment.
H. Fear of Man.
I. Depression.
J. Heaviness.
K. Sorrow.
L. Mourning.
M. Self-pity.
N. Exhibitionism.
O. God-hating.
P. Self-hate.
Q. A false image of God.
R. A false image of self.
S. Fear.
T. Loneliness.
U. Suspicion.
V. Rebellion.

Chapter 6

REBELLION

Every leader, every counselor, every person living has in his life a rebel. These are the people who make Mondays Mondays. They are the ones who challenge every decision you make, who follow your instructions as they see fit, and who in the love of the Lord (of course) misquote every word you utter. They make every board meeting an affair to remember, every counseling session an exercise in frustration, every family reunion a lesson in detente, and (if you are a pastor) make you wish you had an exchange program going with other churches in town.

REBELLION is not only one of the most common problems observed, it is a problem all leaders will experience personally before their death. We not only need to consider those rebellious personalities formed by life experiences, but we must examine those individuals caught in rebellion due to spiritual causes.

For the sake of description, we have taken the liberty of naming the two aspects of the rebellious personality. Type A we will call Gertrude, Type B we will refer to as Gregory. These rebellious personalities usually have their roots in one of two types of life experiences. Depending upon the root of the rebellion, the manner of expression is determined in most cases as follows: The Type A personality is usually noticeably overt in behavior, challenging in attitude and expression, and is the one who will most often lead an open rebellion. The Type B personality has a tendency to be more covert in action, will appear to be the elected leader, and his challenge will come based on either his need or the people's needs.

Type A or Gertrude:

Gertrude's problem with authority, rules and restrictions developed from being under authority figures and rules that were abusive in their power, controlling in their nature, and demeaning and demanding in their attitudes. The product of this is an individual who begins to associate authority figures with deep hurt, loss of identity, oppressive restrictions of her own personality, loss of her own goals, feelings that she is sub-human or evil in nature and an inconvenience to the people around her and can never be trusted to do a positive or right thing. Usually these attitudes are produced because the rules and restrictions established by the authority figures were for the benefit of those authority figures: their own lifestyles, their own goals and as a cover for their own personality defects.

Gertrude is easily recognizable because:

1. She is the one who freely calls you EVERY Monday morning to tell you why your judgments, decisions, and statements of the preceding week were totally erroneous. Or she breezes into your office with a body-language stance which states, "I am here to confront, change, take over or eliminate." In other words, she is openly militant.

2. Gertrude has never been able to sustain a working relationship on any committee or any job, because when she is working under a supervisor she openly debates any direction. If the direction is not changed, she undermines the authority figure, even to the abusive use of slander.

3. She has an innate ability to know which people in a group or congregation can be stirred into strife and contention.

4. Gertrude knows intuitively the weak areas of the leader and can produce an unwise reaction or statement from him to prove her point.

5. She appears arrogant and unbending but the root is always fear and insecurity.

6. Gertrude sees herself as an instrument of punishment

to all authority figures, and therefore she is gratified and encouraged by the leader's discomfort.

Type B or Gregory:

Gregory's problem with authority, rules, and restrictions developed as a result of never being taught to come under any authorities or rules.

1. Either his parents were permissive in nature and felt that using as little negative confrontation and restriction as possible would produce an expressive, well-balanced adult, or that any type of discipline or restraint would repress his creativity.

2. His parents themselves had negative experiences with authority and were afraid they would be abusive in their use of it.

3. The individuals themselves were in some way considered fragile in emotions or physical stamina; or were considered special in either talent or intellect; or had suffered a severe illness that caused the parents to fear for the child's life, or left the child with a permanent scar or defect; or, was born with a handicap or learning disability. These individuals found in Group 3 have been both verbally and nonverbally taught that they are above and undeserving of both restrictions and authority.

Gregory is easily recognizable because:

1. Gregory is the one who calls you on Monday morning with a pouty, pitiful, melancholy explanation as to why the decisions you made do not conform to his intentions in any way whatsoever. If he is confronted, and the leader stands firm, then Gregory will become rigid, judgmental and defiant, basing his actions on a confused state of mind. His next step in manipulation will be open defiance, a stage he will reach only reluctantly.

2. His rebellion often takes the covert form of anguished explanation as to why the rules simply and obviously cannot apply to him.

3. Gregory will often whine and complain about the

unfair attitude displayed by the leader toward him, meanwhile stirring up among the ranks support based on pity and sympathy. His appeal as the underdog becomes a real nuisance because he appears to be fragile and misunderstood.

4. Gregory has the ability to stir rebellion by pointing out the areas in which others in the group are not being correctly cared for in his (and their) opinion. He convinces them that they could do a better job than that being done by those currently in leadership roles.

5. Gregory has an attitude of "You have no right" to correct or change him in any area. Gregory has a stiff-necked, unteachable spirit. He is unresponsive to any logical explanation, no matter how well thought out or presented.

6. Gregory has the ability to express fear of the leader by exaggerating all forms of correction.

7. Gregory never appears to be in control of the rebellion. He always appears to be the appointed spokesperson, and he just never seems to know how he got there.

To further illustrate both personalities, let us look at two different rebellions that occurred in the Bible and separate their root and their expression. We will begin by discussing a rebellion led by a Type A person and relate it to the principles found in the beginning of this chapter.

At this point, stop and read Numbers chapters 16 and 17 to follow the course of rebellion stemming from the root of jealousy and the mistrust of leadership, both often key roots in a Type A personality. In these chapters, you will discover the steps of the rebellion, the leaders' reaction to the rebellion, God's response to rebellion, and the secret that rebellion can seldom be halted once instigated. It can only be dealt with and eliminated individually.

These two chapters exemplify the contagion of rebellion once it is instigated. The rebellion began in the heart of one man, spread to the hearts of three men who (by using principles 2 and 3 of the Type A personality) involved 250 others whose own weaknesses, ambitions, jealousies, and bitterness made them easy targets for involvement. The most alarming fact of rebellion once begun is found in verses 41 thru 50 of chapter 16. After the seed is planted in the hearts of the group as a whole, it can only be eliminated by God directly dealing with individuals, for we read that by morning the entire congregation rose up and accused BOTH Moses and Aaron of murder. All this was due to Satan's ability to invade one person with a spirit of rebellion based on past hurts, jealousies and mistrust of authority.

We find this revolt being led by Korah, Dathan, and Abiram. It is an excellent example of the Type A or Gertrude personality. In verse 3 of Chapter 16, we find the root of the entire rebellion:

> *And they gathered themselves together against Moses and Aaron, and said to them, Ye take too much upon you, seeing all the congregation are holy, every one of them, and the LORD is among them: wherefore then lift ye up yourselves above the congregation of the LORD?*

This one verse serves to illustrate the first three principles of Gertrude's behavior. It would not be at all surprising to learn that the revolt occurred on the first day of the week!

In verse 2 of Numbers 16, we find that Korah blatantly rose up face to face against Moses, and took 250 other leaders with him. When dealing with a Type A personality, you may see a fulfillment of the third principle, since they have no problem trying to be the open leader.

In Numbers 16:12-14 we read the following account:

> *And Moses sent to call Dathan and Abiram, the sons of Eliab: which said, We will not come up:*
>
> *Is it a small thing that thou hast brought us up out of a land that floweth with milk and honey, to kill us in the wilderness, except thou make thyself altogether a prince over us?*
>
> *Moreover thou hast not brought us into a land that*

*floweth with milk and honey, or given us inheritance
of fields and vineyards: wilt thou put out the eyes of
these men? we will not come up.*

When we analyze the contents of these three verses, we
find the elements of principles 2 thru 6 clearly illustrated.
What was occurring was that they were in the process of
openly undermining Moses' position as leader, slandering
his success thus far. We can watch them further the revolt
by knowing the weaknesses of the group and what would
stir that group to strife and contention. They accomplished
it with one simple question:

*Is it a small thing that thou hast brought us up out of a
land that floweth with milk and honey, to kill us in
the wilderness . . .?*

These leaders knew that there was still a yearning for
Egypt in the hearts of Israel, so by reminding them of the
pleasant memories of Egypt they could stir discontent
with present circumstances. We can diagnose the root of
Dathan and Abiran's problem to be mistrust of all authority figures, and a feeling that all authority figures were
abusive in power and controlling in nature, these being
two of the roots of a Type A personality. We can draw this
conclusion from the last phrase of verse 13, which reads:

*. . . except thou make thyself altogether a prince over
us*

and the second-to-last phrase in verse 14, which reads:

. . . wilt thou put out the eyes of these men?

It is easy to see how small, simple phrases spoken BY
the right person, TO the right person, fire latent spirits of
rebellion, discontent and fear.

What a clear picture of principle number 5! We see two
people who are unbending and arrogant expressing their
own fears and insecurities. But when we take verses 13
and 14 in total we see both principles 4 and 6 in full
operation. These two men saw themselves as the instrument of punishment against Moses and Aaron. They had

indeed accomplished principle 4, and we see the following reaction from Moses in verse 15.

> ... and Moses was very wroth, and said unto the LORD, Respect not thou their offering: I have not taken one ass from them, neither have I hurt one of them.

Dathan and Abiram knew that one of the weak areas in Moses' personality was his fear that he would once again commit an unwise act while trying to operate in a place of authority. (Remember the story found in Exodus 3:11-14.) As you can see, these two rebels even used the same descriptive phrase. They further attacked his integrity and his motives for leadership. Isn't it interesting that it took two men only one moment of time to accomplish what all of Israel had not been able to do up until now? This is the first time we do not see Moses standing between God and Israel, but instead giving God free rein to act in judgment against this segment of Israel! But God in His infinite wisdom gave Moses twenty-four hours to cool off, and by verses 20 thru 24 Moses was once again interceding for the nation, and God's judgment fell only on the guilty.

God's only method for treating rebellion in the Old Testament was death. Praise God for the power of the blood of Jesus Christ that gives God another alternative for the treatment of rebellion today! You would think that as the congregation saw the supernatural judgment of God, all future revolts would be cancelled in the hearts of the rebels, but not so. Once the seed of rebellion is sown in a group, each individual must encounter the supernatural involvement of God in his own heart. (Leaders, beware: when murmuring begins, you have no choice but to confront each person who has been involved unwittingly by the rebel. Otherwise you will awaken one Tuesday morning to an entire group of rebels whose sympathy for the person enduring discipline has led them to a revolt of the heart. Beware!)

Now begin reading in Numbers 16:41:

But on the morrow all the congregation of the children of Israel murmured against Moses and against Aaron, saying, Ye have killed the people of the LORD.

Do you see how easy it is for a revolt based on jealousy, ambitions and weaknesses to turn to rebellion of the heart, once discipline has been enforced and the sympathies of the people aroused?

Now let us take a quick look at a rebellion led by a Type B personality and relate it to Type B principles found in the beginning of this chapter. Turn to II Samuel 15:1-13. Here Absalom slowly turned the hearts of the people away from David by the use of principle 4 in the Type B personality. Absalom was always treated as special by those in authority over him because of his beauty and his ability to manipulate their hearts. He actually committed murder in order to even a score, which was to his mind a totally justifiable action.

As we can see, he used the second principle with as much ease as principle 4, because by the time we reach verse 13, the hearts of Israel had been effectively won by him. And yet in presentation to David it appears that Absalom had been elected by the people without his being at all responsible.

And there came a messenger to David, saying, The hearts of the men of Israel are after Absalom.

Upon reviewing verses 1-13, you will notice that Absalom had done everything he could to produce feelings of either love or guilt-induced pity in the hearts of those he ministered to at the gate. Type B personalities very seldom produce feelings of direct hate or revolt against the leader, but instead involve others in the revolt by the use of subtle innuendo. Pause and absorb the truth of the last phrase of verse 6:

so Absalom stole the hearts of the men of Israel.

There are certain traits that both Type A and B

personalities share, so we will briefly describe them as follows:

1. Both groups when faced with continuing authority respond by testing every limit set by the authority figure.

2. Both will attribute negative reasoning and negative benefits to the leader for each decision made.

3. Both will tend to revolt over the most ridiculous issues.

4. Both will continue to follow a course of rebellion, often because they thrive on negative attention.

5. It appears that both are prone to force public disciplinary action against themselves, even when they know it to be untimely for either the group or the leader.

6. A common method of expressing their rebellion is to agree with the leader on first encounter, only to turn and do their own thing when the situation actually arises.

7. Both personality groups are incapable of leadership, even though that is their goal, because they have never learned to follow or to relate to others with whom they work.

I Samuel 15:22-23 makes the clearest statement of God's view of rebellion, while also giving us an indication of the roots of rebellion which we will find in any individual with a rebellious spirit, regardless of whether they are a Type A or B personality. The verses read as follows:

And Samuel said, Hath the Lord as great delight in burnt offerings and sacrifices, as in obeying the voice of the Lord? Behold, to obey is better than sacrifice, and to hearken than the fat of rams.

For rebellion is as the sin of witchcraft, and stubbornness is as iniquity and idolatry. Because thou hast rejected the word of the Lord, he hath also rejected thee from being king.

From the intensity of this passage we understand that God has no alternative but to relieve the rebellious individual of his position or office. Why is it that we find it so difficult to remove a rebellious individual from a place of authority or service until he can receive ministry and healing, when we find the pattern so clearly stated in Scripture? It seems that God views the roots for rebellion and stubbornness in a light which we find severe and unthinkable in our day and age. However, if we spend a moment comparing the results of witchcraft and idolatry to the results of rebellion and stubbornness, we find frightening similarities. For example, all four exist in the worship of any other identity besides the living God. In rebellion and stubbornness we are worshiping self, in witchcraft and idolatry we are worshiping Satan and demons.

Continually, in the Old Testament, God's treatment for rebellion was the same. In Proverbs 17:11 Solomon told us that a cruel messenger would be sent against a rebellious man; Isaiah said (1:19-20) that a rebel will be devoured by the sword for the mouth of the Lord has spoken it. In Ezekiel 20:33-38 God Himself stated that He would purge the rebels out from among Israel.

How grateful we are for the ultimate victory Jesus Christ won for us on Calvary, giving us authority over all the works of the enemy. That victory replaces the sure judgment of the Old Testament with freedom, hope and restoration. What a powerful word we are thus able to offer to those driven and compelled to rebel, whether because of fear, hurt, insecurity or false reality. We can minister to them deliverance from those forces that drive them into rebellious behavior patterns against their will.

With this opportunity comes a four-fold awesome responsibility to the leaders in the body of Jesus Christ:

1. We must be willing to minister deliverance to all those in need.
2. We must be willing to learn all we can about this ministry, as well as how to minister healing in those areas which open the door to the enemy in the first place.
3. We must be willing to learn how to ask the right questions, and discern the prayer needs based on those answers.

4. We must be willing to observe the behavior of people in need of help without being drawn into the strife and contention, and without allowing our emotions to involve us directly with the conflict. (This is the most difficult task of all.)

When dealing with a Type A personality you must ask questions that will reveal the root person (or persons) who through the years has caused the subject to mistrust and to fear all authority. You must further ask questions that will reveal the events which have caused the pain and allowed the spirit of rebellion access to the person's mind, will and emotions. As the person begins to reveal those sources of hurt in his life, you must develop the ability to allow the Holy Spirit to expose those other spirits that accompany that spirit of rebellion. It is not enough, when ministering to a Type A personality, to merely break spirits of rebellion, hatred, strife and contention. If you do not expose (and deliver the person from) other accompanying spirits, you will make it almost impossible for him to stand or to walk in the freedom Jesus Christ brings.

Upon finding the root person involved in such situations, you must break the spirit and power of that person over the individual receiving ministry, by citing the perpetrator by name. (We will give an example of this with the case study of a Type A personality at the end of this section). Next you must break the spirit and power of the perpetrator's negative descriptions of the individual. In a Type A personality you will probably need to get rid of a hurt and wounded spirit, as well as spirits of mistrust or suspicion, spirits of fear, spirits of resentment, spirits of insecurity and spirits of inferiority. Since the Word has already informed us that rebellion is as the sin of witchcraft, and stubbornness is as idolatry, we then must rid the individual of spirits of witchcraft, idolatry and false worship, as well as others the Holy Spirit might reveal at this point.

When dealing with a Type B personality, you must observe whether or not the rebellion stems from the fact that they were never taught to come under authority.

Perhaps their authority figures themselves had problems with authority, and therefore were afraid to administer any type of discipline or restraint, or believed that discipline and restraint would restrict the child's creativity. Other causes for this personality could be that this person was special in talent or ability, or had a handicap or possibly had a life-threatening illness. Once you have discerned which of these is the source, then you must ask questions that will reveal which spirits are accompanying the spirit of rebellion. You may find that there are spirits of pride, arrogance, or superiority. In other situations, it may be a spirit of anarchy. It may, on the other hand, stem from a need to punish others. In addition, never forget when dealing with this person to eliminate the spirits of witchcraft, idolatry and any others in this grouping which the Holy Spirit might reveal.

Now that we have considered two types of the most common ways in which rebellious personalities can be formed from life experiences, let us look at spiritual causes that can produce the same result. Remember that these experiences may not deteriorate into being roots of a rebellious personality immediately. However, as the person continues in these areas of sin, it can happen eventually.

A. Direct involvement in occult practices, or receiving help, information, direction, or relief in times of trouble or need from someone directly involved in occult practices.

B. Participation in any and all forms of false worship.

C. Involvement in areas of direct compromise with God's law, or of premeditated sin.

D. Decisions made to go against God's known direction in areas of 1) employment, 2) relationships, 3) value expressions, 4) refusal to use spiritual gifts given by God, 5) decisions to counter any direction God has given to a person as a leader for the group.

E. Rebellion to those in spiritual authority without just, moral, or spiritual cause.

In the process of considering the effects of occult involvement, we must realize that we were made by our Creator in such a complex manner that if we allow a spiritual disease or infection to take hold of our spiritual man, every aspect of our personality is soon affected. Even our reactions to situations and to people begin to be affected. Have you ever noticed that people who are engaged in battle with God are irritable, and tend to fight with everyone and everything? Nothing seems to please them, and you can do *nothing* correctly, including staying out of their way.

Some people express their internal unrest by fighting every decision made by those around them. You become their target just by being in the vicinity. If you commit the "unpardonable sin" of being at peace with God, or share something He has shown you or done for you, there is no bomb shelter deep enough or secure enough to keep you a safe distance from their tongue! Rebellion against God transforms normally cooperative and helpful people into contentious and rebellious personalities. This is particularly true if the rebellion in progress involves occult practices. Thus the reasons why rebellion is considered by God as a serious and destructive sin become clear. The rebellion involving occult practices gives manipulative and controlling powers to those involved in occult practices. This type of rebellion has power to poison the spirit, the soul and also the body, even unto death. This is better realized when we consider the fact that sin first entered time through Satan's rebellion.

In Isaiah 14:12-19 and in Ezekiel 28:12-19, God pulled back the curtain of time and showed the archangel Lucifer's revolt. God's response was not only instant judgment but also His ultimate judgment. God has a plan for Satan and for those who have, and will, join forces with him. In I Samuel 15:23, Samuel was explaining to King Saul why God's judgment would be so severe against him, and gave us the truth that witchcraft births rebellion. Rebellion births stubbornness. And stubbornness births idolatry. Therefore, you should well know that there is NO harmless divination, NO good white magic, NO innocent astrology chart. Satan tries to accomplish the same things today that he did in the very beginning. He wants to control the mind, the will and the emotions of man, God's special creation, and to manipulate man's worship and responses to his Father.

In considering the effect of false worship, as in statement B, please turn to Exodus 32. The people became impatient and fearful at the delay God brought into their lives. They decided that for their own best interest they should replace Jehovah with another god. (Is it possible that we, like they, do not trust God? When delays and difficulties come, would we seek an alternate god who would be more prone to operate in the way WE demand?) Not only was rebellion the result, but in verse 6 we read:

And they rose up early on the morrow, and offered the burnt offerings, and brought peace offerings; and the people sat down to eat and drink, and rose up to play.

In verse 25 of the same chapter, it is further revealed that the people were in such a frenzy of drunkenness and false worship that they were naked. Do you not find it interesting that the same state occurred in the Garden of Eden when Adam and Eve chose to worship themselves rather than their Creator? Rebellion which births false worship births lasciviousness and unrighteousness.

As the events continued, God told Moses in verses 7-10 the way He viewed the results:

1. God no longer called them His people but Moses' people.
2. God now saw them as corrupted.
3. God felt that they had turned quickly and completely out of His way.
4. God viewed them as giving Satan credit for His own action.

5. God said they were stiff-necked. (Remember the words of Samuel to Saul, *"Rebellion is as the sin of witchcraft."*)

God had a cure in mind: "Let me kill them and start over with you, Moses"! God's judgment for the sin was that the tribe of Levi had the gruesome task of killing 3000 men who did not repent. In verse 35, we read, *"And the LORD plagued the people, because they made the calf, which Aaron made."*

The most obvious example of statement C is found in the life of King David. In II Samuel 11 we find David at home instead of out to war where he should have been. As a result he was not sleeping well, got up and looked out the window, saw a lovely woman bathing, found out that she was married, knew God's law but committed adultery with her anyway. As a result they conceived a child. And because of his refusal to confess his sin, he was forced to commit a third sin to cover up the first two. When God did not allow the sin to be covered, David, still not wanting his sin to be exposed, had Joab arrange for the death of her husband. Sad as it may be, rebellion against God's laws always expands and often affects yet more people. In I Corinthians 5:6, Paul said, *". . . . Know ye not that a little leaven leaveneth the whole lump?"*

Let us dissect David's rebellion. Lust birthed covetousness. Covetousness birthed adultery. Adultery birthed lying. Lying birthed murder. The end result was that the lives of four people were affected to such an extent that their life courses were altered forever. In II Samuel 12:10-14, we find the following judgments:

. . . the sword would never depart from David's house.
. . . David's wives would be taken by another man before his very eyes and another man would lie with them out in the open sun.

(The second was fulfilled by his own son Absalom when

he revolted against David and took control of the government. He lay with David's wives on the rooftop of the palace.)

The law of God will not be violated, nor its ramifications altered. The sin of the father was found in the son, and the promise in the book of Luke that the sin done in private would be exposed in public was fulfilled. Again—God stated that the child they had conceived in sin would die.

The rebellions named in statement D above are numerous enough, as well as specific enough, to cause you to draw from your own frame of reference. These are areas affecting everyday living and everyday choices. It bears repeating that God will ALWAYS bring you to Himself in the easiest way you will come. Our God has a habit of bringing you out of what you feel is your safety or comfort zone, and He loves to violate your theology that does not agree with His!

Chapter 7

ADDICTIONS AND COMPULSIONS

Pastors and leaders may have a strong desire to skip this chapter as elements of it may sound frighteningly like looking in a bathroom mirror, or at a TV monitor of your board or leadership council meetings. We're going to look at both a compulsive and an addictive personality. The compulsive personalities are usually the people who, when they first join a church or group, cause such an excitement and thrill. The leaders feel as though God has given them a gold mine, but soon discover that what they really have is possibly a runaway train. The problems begin when it is realized that this personality has an insatiable appetite for work. Accomplishment, perfection, new ideas, programs and growth consume them constantly to the exclusion of all else. For example, these are the people who call you with a better idea than yours at least once a day and have no realization that not everything can be done—"It only takes a moment." If you are the "leader" and have any of these problems *yourself*, havoc is the result. One of the following situations comes into existence:

A. Every other committee member quits.
B. They become so frustrated that they feel they cannot measure up and hard feelings are the result.
C. You and the super train end up doing everything, producing a church (or group) of spectators.

This is extremely unhealthy for the group as it makes

for a leadership vacuum that will in the end make the group so top-heavy that it falls over with any extra new growth. It also produces such overwork for the few compulsive personalities that either burnout or a "Messiah Complex" results. They begin to feel that if they do not do all the work, either it will not get done, or it will not be done correctly, creating a false sense that everything will come to a halt without them.

As we attempt to help you recognize either a compulsive or addictive personality, please bear in mind that not everyone will have every trait delineated in this chapter. The absence of some of the traits does not mean that the person is neither compulsive nor addictive. It merely means his personality has not advanced as far into the problem as it could! The absence of some of the symptoms does not eliminate the person's need for ministry, nor does it lessen his need for prompt ministry.

The compulsive and the addictive personalities share many root causes, and those not jointly shared are very closely related. Hence, when closely examined, it is no longer confusing as to how one child in the same family becomes compulsive and the other addictive. For the sake of easier reading we will name the compulsive personality Jackie and the addictive personality Jack. We will consider the compulsive personality first.

Let us begin by viewing Jackie's compulsive personality traits, which society sees as positive. Then we will examine those traits and some of the problems that can and do arise from them. Jackie tends to be one or more of the following:

A. Workaholic.
B. Perfectionist.
C. Compulsive cleaner.
D. Compulsively orderly.
E. Punctual.
F. Highly regimented.

G. Preoccupied with personal appearance.
H. Driven to achievement and accomplishment.
I. Driven to developing new and different ways of doing things.
J. Over-involved in causes and groups.

Now that we have outlined the most common symptoms of Jackie's personality, let us go back and analyze the by-products which could be found in each category.

A. Workaholic.

Out of the workaholic pattern stems the need for more and more success, and the attainment of more and more levels of knowledge in diversified subject matter. This is seen when Jackie, no matter what subject is being discussed, has studied it and is compelled to share with you every piece of information she has ever learned. (Confusion can arise here because this is also a symptom of the compulsive talker, at whom we will take a quick look later.) As a workaholic, Jackie feels a need to produce a greater volume of work this week than last week. She has great difficulty sitting still and finds it difficult, if not impossible, to allow herself to take a day off, or have a period of time in which she is doing nothing productive. When questioned, all Jackie can explain is that she either feels so guilty, or thinks that doing nothing is a waste of time. If honest she will admit that when forced to sit still she feels like she will come out of her skin, or start screaming. These are the people about whom you find yourself saying, "They just aren't any fun," or "They have no idea how to play."

B. Perfectionist.

From the perfectionist's traits the following expressions are usually observed:

1. She feels that any error on her part detracts from who she is as a person.
2. She cannot allow mistakes in anyone who works with her, for it reflects directly on her own personal worth.

She feels that another's error makes her less of a person, since to be a normal or respected individual one must be perfect. She will reach a point where she feels that she should do everything herself to avoid problems. This seems to stem from the fear that if all is not perfect people will neither love nor respect her. Sometimes Jackie has vaguely disturbing thoughts that she must constantly compensate for something seriously lacking within herself. She often feels that she cannot get by with what everyone else can, unfair as that may be, which leaves her frustrated and confused.

C. Compulsive cleaner.

Closely related to the perfectionist and usually an expression of the same trait is the compulsive cleaner. This is shown when Jackie cleans repeatedly the same areas even when there is no need. Eventually, Jackie will be emptying and cleaning ash trays while they are being used.

D. Compulsively orderly.

The individual who is compulsively orderly surpasses the cleaner in that this trait not only deals with the cleanliness of her environment, but the orderliness of her work area while working, and the appearance of everything she presents or produces. Jackie's office is perfectly arranged, even down to the books on the shelves in size order. She has difficulty working with others who do not maintain her standard of order.

E. Compulsively punctual.

When Jackie becomes compulsively punctual she is completely controlled by the clock. Spontaneity becomes impossible without causing a nervous reaction within her. She will also have difficulty dealing with an emergency or an unplanned schedule change, because they will seem unimportant, or of a different nature than what is already planned.

F. Highly regimented.

The highly regimented character trait is basically the

same as the preceding one except that Jackie's sense of security is usually wrapped up in the sameness of her schedule.

G. Preoccupied with personal appearance.

When Jackie becomes compelled to be perfect in her appearance (for example, with exercise, makeup, color choices, hair, etc.) she can reach the point where she can be seen by no one until all is up to her standards. All her free time is spent improving and maintaining her appearance. At this stage a controlling fear of growing older begins to take over.

The next two categories are so closely related that we will examine them together.

H. Driven to achievement and accomplishment.

I. Developing new and different ways of doing things.

When driving needs for either achievement or accomplishment begin to consume Jackie's complete thought processes, we say she is highly motivated or upwardly mobile. There is usually no problem with this attitude until everything and everyone is suddenly expendable to accomplish her next goal. The other outlet for this trait is constantly finding and developing new hobbies. This habit seems to fill the driving need for personal improvement as well as the urgent need for knowledge of, and involvement with, new things. This personality has a tendency to bore quickly, therefore needing new victories to combat low self-esteem.

J. Over-involved in causes and groups.

The intensity of Jackie's involvement with each new cause or group can only be compared to the dedication of Don Quixote and the force of a whirlwind. All of her workaholic tendencies surface, her Messianic drives take control and she is single-handedly out to change the world. Her entire life becomes so submerged in each new venture that everything else suffers. She wants to change everything being done if she can find a better way to accomplish the goal. Her own identity is lost to the cause or group. She will take on as much work as will be released to her, at first being loved by all but gradually being resented by more and more of those who have been involved longer than she. If she should assume leadership of the group or cause, she can not help demanding more and more from everyone else without understanding their limitations.

Traits found on the negative side of the compulsive personality are not often described as being compulsive in nature, so they are usually lumped into the addictive pile. Let us take a good look at some that seem to fit with the compulsive root.

1. Compulsive talker.
2. Compulsive shopper.
3. Compulsive saver.
4. Compulsive eater.

A. Compulsive talker.

These people talk out of need for a defense mechanism. They feel that if they allow anyone to get too close to them, their true selves will be exposed as people to be disliked. Keeping the floor and controlling the conversation keep them in control and others at a safe distance.

B. Compulsive shopper.

These people shop regularly because they are driven to buy for at least some of the following reasons:

1. To improve their image.
2. To satisfy that aspect of themselves that bores quickly.
3. To prove that they are good with money and know how to get a good deal.
4. To satisfy their need for security and position.
5. Out of fear of deprivation.
6. As a form of escapism.
7. For euphoric gratification.

Compulsive shoppers usually need to go into a mall or

store every few days, spend hours looking, intimately feeling and observing every article. They then buy things they do not need or already have in abundance. If we could invade their closets and cabinets we would find articles of clothing hanging with the tags still on them. We would find shoes scarcely (if ever) worn, and other items in abundance never used and probably not even unpackaged. Some of the people in this category find it necessary to purchase a multitude of labor-saving devices, and/or the newest forms of entertainment. Many of these things are never used more than once or twice and they are purchased merely because they are available.

C. Compulsive saver.

The compulsive savers are people who are afraid to throw anything away lest it be needed down the line and have to be repurchased. They would then be guilty of imprudence. They are incapable of throwing things out because it would separate them from their past and threaten their value and identity in the present.

D. Compulsive eater.

The compulsive eaters are those who eat to relieve pressure, frustration, fear, loneliness, anxiety, rejection or failure. They also eat to celebrate joy, success, a new relationship, a special event or to provide a sense of security and well being. NOTE: These are the same causes for the use of any addictive substances!

Since the root causes for the compulsive and addictive personalities are usually the same, the differences appear to be the expressions chosen by the persons to display and get relief from the driving forces inside of them. In a family of two or more childen, some members may be compulsive while others may be addictive, but none of the children will be without driving forces to some degree.

One of the most famous comic strips today has made its main character an appealing caricature of an addictive and compulsive personality. He is such a well-loved cat because his creator has taken those traits buried within us, developed them and made us laugh at ourselves. Much can be learned from his own frustrations concerning his inability to control his behavior, or reactions to his environment.

An addictive personality is easily involved in anything that produces:

1. Euphoric highs or periods of anesthetic living, in which no emotional pain of present or past is felt.
2. Periods of freedom from stress or mental pain.
3. Freedom from reality.

Addictive substances are things which repeatedly satisfy one or more of the senses while altering the individual's concept of reality. The most common addictive substances are as follows: alcohol, drugs, nicotine, caffeine, food (especially sugar products) and chocolate. (Chocolate is separated from sugar products because the addiction appears to be more to the chemical in the cocoa bean itself than to the sugar.) Last in this category is adrenalin. We have separated it from other substances because it is not consumed, but produced by the individual. People in this category are addicted to crisis, and tend to create a crisis because of their dependence on regular doses of adrenalin in their systems. Adrenalin is not only produced by crisis situations, but it is also released at times of heavy workloads and short deadlines. It is therefore possible to classify someone a workaholic who is really an adrenalin junkie.

As can be observed from the preceding description, most addictions supply a secondary need for oral gratification while satisfying the senses and altering concepts.

Another aspect of the addictive personality is a tendency to use different forms of escapism to cope with life situations and demands beyond the addict's level of coping mechanisms. Addicts also use escapism to avoid making decisions or to avoid people who are too taxing. As the person uses escapism as a defense, the following dangerous side effects often develop:

A. The tool takes control of the person, and even when he might desire to remain involved in a situation, the person finds himself automatically escaping.
B. His ability to correctly perceive not only his own environment, but the people in his environment, and their motives, becomes greatly impaired, thereby affecting both his judgment and ability to act.
C. The need to escape pain becomes so great, and the need for a euphoric sense of well-being so necessary, that the individual will spare no expense to satisfy the addiction, as well as to escape into whatever form of fantasy environment he creates best.

The most common escapes addicts indulge in are as follows:

A. Gambling. It produces a euphoric sense of well-being, whether the individual is winning or losing. It is also an addictive form of escape.
B. Flights of fantasy. This includes two types of individuals, the person who always finds himself daydreaming at high points of stress, worry, or boredom, and the individual who is always on stage as either the natural actor or comedian.
C. Entertainment junkie. The person who uses a form of entertainment to escape, such as TV, books or movies. This person is so addicted to these entertainment forms that he will be spending his time engaged in these forms of entertainment at the expense of all else. When questioned, the response is usually that he uses the entertainment both to unwind and to accomplish some sense of well-being.
D. The compulsive storyteller. This person writes fictional stories to gain relief in his own life.
E. The compulsive liar. (This is the person who cannot separate truth from fiction.) This individual will literally progress to a point at which he is not lying in his own mind—he is telling the truth as he

sees it. In many cases, he will even be able to pass a lie-detector test.

There are two forms of sexual addiction, both producing physical gratification and a chemical high. The first is the addiction to masturbation. This individual is compelled to lengthy periods of self-gratification that become so fulfilling that he no longer needs or requires a sexual partner. This individual knows how to accomplish fulfillment of his own sexual urges, and his accompanying need for increasing pain which masturbation generates. Masturbation is an addiction that also produces a side effect of euphoria. As this form of addiction continues, however, the individual can no longer be gratified by a sexual partner, as the partner no longer is capable of fulfilling his needs.

The second form of sexual addiction is the individual who requires an unusually high frequency of sexual activity. He may or may not require a different partner with each contact, but he does have a driving need for variety, both in positions and partners. Very often these people require gratification by using various sexual devices, and their desires are heightened with oral and/or visual stimulation.

Now let us consider another form of addiction, sleep. There are people who are addicted to sleep, not just as an escape, but as an addictive means to produce a false sense of well-being. This is the person who falls so quickly to sleep during a time of stress that it becomes a fascination to those around him. Some mistakenly label him as either lazy or unable to grasp the severity of the situations within his environment. Neither of these labels is correct. It is merely that, as the person experiences more and more stress, his coping mechanism is to retreat into a state perceived to be safe and secure. His hope is that when he awakens eveything will be all right. Therefore sleep does the same for him that drugs and alcohol do for others.

A compulsive and/or addictive personality has been the source of much debate in professional circles for many years. The debate has raged over whether these personalities were learned, created or inherited. The professionals who held the viewpoint that these personalities were primarily inherited have recently received encouragement. Scientific research data has been released showing that upon testing different family units, a similar EEG pattern was found among those families whose members were addictive personalities. Even members of these families who had never even tried an addictive substance had EEG patterns identical to the family members who were addicted. Without an understanding of the material presented in the chapters of this book regarding iniquity, this would be the most alarming scientific data discovered in the last twenty years. It would open the door for many controversial debates over methods of eliminating such influences from our society for the purpose of improving the race. However, due to the Biblical truth concerning iniquity passed down to the third and fourth generations, it is instead the most encouraging evidence discovered to date to support the fact that God loves man so much that He provided a way of freedom even from those things inherited.

An addictive-compulsive personality is one of the most common personalities to be observed regularly in family lines from generation to generation. How many times have you heard yourself say, "That family always has an alcoholic or compulsive eater," or, "That person is a workaholic just like his dad"? This is why so much debate has raged as to whether personalities are inherited or trained by environment. Data seems to indicate that if one or both of the parents are addicted to a substance, or have a strong compulsive problem, ALL of the children will fight tendencies toward compulsions both positive and negative, or will fight addiction to a substance or activity. The basic reasoning behind this statement has been that the children learn by observation, or are shaped by the parents' positive reinforcement for certain personality traits. However, the Bible states that the truth is found locked up in iniquity.

The addictive-compulsive personality seems to be accompanied by an intense feeling of inferiority, a fear of rejection and a high sense of feeling unacceptable. Some professionals have gone so far as to suggest that part of the motivational formation of the addictive and compulsive personalities is their feeling that they are not loved for their own merit, and must therefore compensate. When they realize that the standard they perceive for being loved is unattainable by them, their level of frustration and despair rises. From their desperate feelings of inability to cope with life, they become addicted to something, or become so compulsive as to develop an over-competent defense that keeps all people at a safe distance.

This personality usually has an extra area of frustration and fear. This is due to their feeling that they will never succeed, or overcome, their own family reputation if it is a negative one, nor measure up if it is a positive compulsive one. Most of these people have been placed in one of the following situations during formative periods of their development, or during times of extreme vulnerability when their personalities were fragile enough to be altered:

1. Authority figures set standards too high for them to attain.
2. They were made to feel responsible for the lives of other people at much too young an age.
3. They have usually been taught to fear being classified as a loser.
4. It was constantly reinforced that they were inherently evil, lazy or stupid.

Children of an addictive parent are usually given a mixed message. They are taught to achieve, achieve, achieve, until the children exceed the parents' own potential, or the parents become threatened by that possibility. The parent then turns upon the child and psychologically abuses him for the very achievements he has accomplished at the parent's insistence! This creates an ambivalent nature which sets the child up for either intense confusion or rage. At this point, depending on the expression developed by the child, he will either become a compulsive individual always trying to prove his own worth, or an addicted individual trying to erase the ongoing pain and frustration from his emotions. Another method used by an addictive parent to halt the child's success will be accusation against the child for having an arrogant view of himself. If this approach is the one used, the parent or authority figure will usually go out of his way to remind the child of the family's reputation in the town or community.

Shame and guilt are the next elements that seem to strongly shape the children of addictive parents. These two traits are intrinsic to the addictive personality. It seems that the children of addictive parents are made to feel by others that their parents' behavior casts a reflection on the children's own basic nature. Most people make them feel that it will only be a matter of time until their behavior is just like that of their parents. This attitude, therefore, makes the children feel that they were born inherently bad or unacceptable to society. They have spent their years trying to overcompensate for those feelings of shame, guilt, unworthiness and evil. When those efforts of overcompensation do not work, they find themselves addicted to a substance or activity that helps them forget, or acts as an anesthetic to block the emotional pain.

The third strong element in the formation of the personality of a child of an addictive parent is fear—of confrontation, violence and criticism. This produces an unteachable adult who feels that every form of correction or instruction is control, manipulation or being consumed by an authority figure. This child becomes so fearful of failure that he will find an escape into a substance or activity, the only way to handle the continual pain he feels. Most of them seem to feel that the starkness and the struggle of life can never be alleviated without some tool or anesthetic.

The fourth element that can shape the personality of the child of an addictive parent is compelled denial and an intricate fantasy woven to protect the parent or parents. As a result, this child has tremendous difficulties separating fantasy from reality. He grows up with a complex denial system. This produces a tendency toward paranoia, and if a detailed family history is not taken, a person deep into this response can be confused with someone suffering from a classic paranoid personality. Sometimes this child is taught, in the process of the protective denial of the non-addictive parent, that the other parent's addiction is due to the behavior, or the personality, of the child. By the time the child reaches adulthood, there has been produced in him such a fear that he is so intrinsically bad that he can never admit any error or failure, no matter how small.

The children of compulsive parents are also encouraged to achieve, achieve, achieve, but when that achievement becomes the thing that the children are preoccupied with, the parents then turn around, and in the best interest of the children encourage a more well-rounded lifestyle (e.g., sports, socials, music). This often produces children who are as compulsive at play as they are at work and other activities.

For a child of a compulsive parent, the shame and guilt that shape their personality stem from the fact that they feel that they will never achieve the level of perfection or success that the parent has set for them. Therefore, they feel they were born inherently defective or weak, and they must spend more and more time overcompensating in one area or another. The other aspect that can create the guilt, shame and a sense of worthlessness is when the child feels that it was his fault that the parent had to be so often absent from the home.

Also, the children of compulsive parents are shaped by a need for a denial or fantasy state because of standards being set above their capability to achieve. Therefore they are forced to deny and fantasize their level of failure and/or achievement. As an adult, these children may fall into a Messiah Complex, which forces everyone in their environment to be dependent on them, and every project to demand their explicit instruction and attention.

Children of compulsive parents are reared with an ongoing fear of never making it, of never being good enough, of always causing ongoing disappointment and embarassment to the parent. They become adults who are compelled to overcompensate or overachieve. By adulthood, they are compulsive learners, and feel that they must have something to say on every subject in order to be considered worthy. These adults find taking criticism or instruction as threatening to them as do the children of addictive parents because it opens those wounds of constant inferiority and rejection.

Therefore, when ministering to either a compulsive or addictive personality, some of the same needs will be present. Be sure to break the spirit and power of the parents. It is impossible to give a cut-and-dried list of spirits that will always be present, or an ironclad method of ministry. But, once the family lines are broken, some suggestions are certainly possible.

A. Rejection.
B. Fear.
C. Unworthiness.
D. Shame.
E. Guilt.
F. Inferiority.
G. Evil.
H. Rage, anger, hate.
I. Addiction (Be sure to address the ones involved).
J. Dependence.
K. Compulsion.
L. Hurt and wounded.
M. False reality, flights of fantasy, denial.
N. Failure and fear of failure.
O. False self-image.

At this point the individuals need a great deal of inner healing, and a major adjustment in the way they see and understand themselves. It would be a good idea to pray with them that God not only heal their memories and emotions, but also their concept of themselves.

As is always true of the newly delivered believer, there should be a spiritual family to walk beside him and nurture him for a season. Thought patterns become habits too, and while the driving forces are now gone, habits take time to break. We suggest much tender care, perhaps even a cadre of helpers whose privileges and responsibilities are strengthening others.

Chapter 8

INTRODUCTION TO VICTIMS AND THE ABUSER

In the next few chapters we will address a serious problem that seems to be surfacing in our society on all levels and in all sections as never before, that of abuse. It does not appear logical that this is simply an effect of abuse being reported more often due to better education, more public awareness, and more resources available to help. It does, however, seem that as society and the family are malfunctioning more and more, the moral fiber of our homes is fraying and the problem is more widespread. We will attempt in these next few chapters to discuss aspects of child, psychological, physical, sexual and spouse abuse. Then we will take a look at the abuser and what made him reach the point where there was a freedom to misuse and abuse another human being.

Our further goal is to make you, as a leader, aware of those in your group or church who are in need of your help, your ministry. You will need to be able to recognize them by their behavior patterns, attitudes, body language and mode of dress. Further, we would like to give you an understanding of their responses to certain situations by giving you a glimpse into their emotions and thought processes.

Of those individuals experiencing abuse in one form or another, those being subjected to either incest or molestation are less likely to volunteer the information and request help. Therefore you must become extremely sensitive to the Holy Spirit as well as alert to the many warning signs. In these forms of abuse the victims themselves are so ashamed, and feel that there is something so evil about their person, that they will have difficulty admitting the existence of the problem even to their pastors or counselors. Do not let this deter you from questioning them, making an attempt to bring the situation to light, in order to minister help. You must be very gentle, always emphasizing that the problem has nothing to do with their character, and is neither a reflection on them nor a statement against them. You MUST have them understand that their secret will remain just that, but that Jesus Christ came to earth to set free such captives as they have become. You are offering them a hope they never knew.

Most victims of this type of abuse deny the reality of it for as many years as possible, even into adulthood. Then their statement usually will be that while the abuse was in progress they went into such a state of denial that they just were "not there" while the act was in progress. As the victims grow up, the most common defense mechanism they use to protect their own sanity, as well as their sense of well-being, is amnesia.

In most cases, the amnesia is so total that no real memory of childhood remains, or the memories are so distorted that they actually believe that everything was PERFECT. As you can well understand, this puts even more pressure on the victims. They can find no logical explanation for their problems, behaviors, fears, reactions or dreams. It will also force you, who are ministering to them, to depend on the Holy Spirit for His direction and His help.

The rewards of receiving ministry for these wounded so far exceed their wildest dreams that we strongly urge you to expend yourselves on their behalf. God has granted to you His own power to bring His own truth into their lives and set them marvelously free. May He guide you into His truth as you obey Him.

Chapter 9

INCEST AND MOLESTATION

Neither this chapter, nor the ones to follow, are intended to be exhaustive treatises. We will discuss only the symptoms observed most frequently and the feelings and fears most often expressed by the victims themselves. Our main goal is to teach how the different personalities are formed, how to recognize the problems, and how to minister to the individuals. Therefore, we have devoted less space to describing the symptoms themselves. More specific symptoms will be discussed in the section dealing with fears.

It must also be stated that the symptoms of the victim personality and the symptoms of the battered-child syndrome vary. These variances may be based on the severity of the abuse experienced, the frequency of the abuse, the victim's reaction to the abuse, and the progression of the disorder. Not all symptoms will appear with each case. Another phenomenon must be noted for consideration: If a woman who was neither molested nor victimized by incest while growing up is raped (by an assailant or by her husband), she may develop the same symptoms.

Please remember that the effect of sexual abuse varies by the amount of trauma each victim individually experienced and the internal strength of the victim. Therefore, we will go from the least affected to the most severely affected without painstakingly describing the shades of effect in between.

PHYSICAL APPEARANCE.

It is usually possible to describe the physical appearance

of an individual who has experienced some form of sexual abuse as follows:

A. Clothing. Before these victims have been severely affected, their clothes are entirely different from those they may choose in the severe stage. In the early stages, these victims simply want to reduce the amount of attention drawn to themselves. Their clothing can be best described as non-descript, avoiding vivid or saturated colors. Fashions will never be flashy, but tailored, and always slightly out of style. They will never identify themselves with a certain style of dress. They will never set the standard of dress for their friends or peers.

As the symptoms of this disorder intensify, their clothing will become unflattering, poorly fitted, probably wrinkled, always de-emphasizing the human form and making it as unappealing as possible. Their clothing may also convey an attitude of poverty, even though that could be far from truth. At this point the internal stress, consciously or not, has reached such an intensity that they have no excess strength to maintain a non-descript expression. Most of their emotional energy is now being expended to keep their emotional and behavioral reactions in balance. Their clothing seems to shout, "I don't like myself and I feel worthless." The colors they choose will be uncoordinated, if not mismatched. Victims at this stage will make poor choices of fabric combinations and may mix articles of clothing that will be considered fashion errors. For example, they may wear white work socks with dress shoes or a plaid sports shirt under a suit. Women at this stage will tend to wear high necklines and long sleeves. There may be a lack of concern in both sexes for personal cleanliness, as well as a lack of concern that clothing be properly maintained.

The exception to this is those whose response to the abuse has been to become extremely sexually active. These usually dress for the purpose of eliciting a sexual response from others.

B. Hair. As in the description above, the degree of the effect of the trauma can be determined by the hairstyle and by the overall appearance. As physical abuse begins, they do NOT want people looking at them. You may sense that their hair becomes a "mask" that they can hide behind. In this early stage, they may well choose ordinary and unflattering hairstyles. Typically, by the time they have reached the most intensely affected stage, their hair will appear oily and unkempt, poorly styled, and inappropriate for their age. Often they will complain that their hair requires too much time and energy to be maintained properly. Their hair will probably hang in their face or be long and straight on the sides. You will definitely realize that they are now hiding behind their hair. At this stage, there will be no attempt to keep up with modern styles, or any style flattering to their features. Once again, the exception to this description is the individual whose response to the abuse has been to become extremely sexually active.

C. Physical presence. In the beginning stages of this disorder, you may observe something so slight that the victims just do not appear "right." Their body language will convey attitudes of fear and worthlessness, showing contempt for themselves. As the effects increase, you will begin to notice an appearance that has been described by some as a gray pallor—an almost indescribable color. The women will usually wear little or no make-up at any time. The men may well be careless shavers, or their appearance may in some other way state their feelings of worthlessness and unattractiveness. Subconsciously, unattractiveness is the message they are trying to transmit, because in that state is safety. If they are not viewed as appealing, they may never again have to fear being violated. Men tend not to bathe as often as they should, and to wear soiled or wrinkled clothing. Both men and women will tend to feel they are "dirty." By way of contrast, a few will express this feeling of being "dirty" by being compulsive in their need for cleanliness. Some may even bathe several times a day, changing clothes each time.

Both men and women may fight an unending battle with being overweight, unless they receive help in behavioral modification from a weight-control group or from a chemical substance.

It must be pointed out that since most victims of incest or molestation have little or no memory, the thought processes that produce their behavior and govern their choices are subconscious. They do not understand why they look like they do, nor do they have a conscious memory of any event which they can blame. Therefore, this lack causes them more frustration and induces more feelings of inferiority, convincing them there is something innately wrong with them. It has been noted that some victims at this stage believe that their real person is locked up inside and cannot get out. They are quite sure, however, that if they COULD escape they would be competent and very likable. Once again, the same exception exists: it seems that those who respond to sexual abuse by being extremely sexually active can best be described as total opposites in all of the above categories.

D. Physical environment. In the early stages of the formation of victim personalities, most victims will find it easier to keep those areas in their homes or offices that are seen by the public cleaner than their private areas. They are, at this point, able to enlist help of some sort to keep their environment clean. However, as the disorder intensifies, they become almost incapable of enlisting help, as they see themselves unworthy of assistance. Their environment actually overwhelms them, and their homes and offices will become extremely cluttered and disorganized. Simultaneously, their homes and offices will be uniquely decorated with colors and furniture that make the statement "This area is unloved." Their work areas or desks will be loaded down and disorganized, seemingly an outward expression of inner confusion and emotional change.

E. Sleep habits. They will usually wear layers of clothing to bed and find it almost, if not totally, impossible to sleep without covers of some sort, regardless of the temperature. They will usually prefer their beds to be placed up against a wall on at least one side. If the room cannot be arranged accordingly, they will make one side of the bed as inaccessible as possible and will sleep on that side. If they are not married, they will take books and other articles to bed with them and fall asleep with those things in their bed. They will usually sleep facing the door and may find it difficult to sleep without a small light on. They will always sleep on the edge of the bed as though to limit accessibility.

Sexual victims will either be prone to poor sleep habits, often suffering from nightmares, or will sleep so soundly that they always seem to be in a state of deep sleep. They may remember their nightmares, because they are so traumatic in nature, but they will never remember ordinary dreams. They may very often wake up with a sense that they did dream, but are incapable of recalling it. They will blame this dreamlessness on the fact that they sleep so deeply. More often than not, they will wake up more tired than when they went to bed.

One trait shared by both physically and sexually abused victims is that if anyone walks into their room, they are immediately awakened. The significance of this behavior is better understood when we remember that these victims usually have no conscious memory of the attacks suffered while growing up. Therefore they do not understand their motives for behaving as they do. It is further significant since they NEVER compare behavior with other victims. ·

F. Body language. These victims usually maintain wide territorial spaces and become immediately uncomfortable if their comfort zones are invaded. This will hold true even if the invader has been known for a long period of time and the level of relationship has purportedly become deep enough to trust the invader. They do not like being touched, particularly being hugged. They hate being confined and work hard at positioning themselves so they will not be hemmed in or be vulnerable in any way. If they do permit themselves to be touched, they are never relaxed. Their rigid posture communicates the fact that they are merely "putting up" with such attention. They are ALWAYS alert to any movement in their peripheral vision.

A female who has been repeatedly victimized will tend to sit in a protected position, legs crossed and usually wrapped round her ankles. Sometimes she will even protect herself more by placing her hand between her legs. The male will also sit in protected positions; very seldom will he have freedom to sit with his legs apart.

EMOTIONAL STATUS.

The psychological description of sexually abused individuals is more complicated and difficult to break down into easy-to-read paragraphs. So let us begin by laying a foundation for the damage to the emotions.

Since the Bible clearly informs us that God has written on the hearts of all mankind His basic laws and standards, there is within all of us at birth a built-in system of right and wrong. WE call that system conscience, and, as all of us have come to know, it has the most uncanny way of going off at the most inopportune moments, ruining all our fun—or so we think. Accepting its existence, let us proceed. A child who, while under the care of an adult, is not only violated in his own body but is forced to violate God's law, is open to an intense amount of emotional damage, as well as spiritual contamination. God takes this problem so seriously that there are TWENTY laws against incest in the Bible, and the apostle Paul brought an entire church under discipline over this sin. In Leviticus 20:11-12, God's view of that sin is brought into sharper focus as He emphasizes the importance of those twenty commands by levying a sentence of DEATH for the sin of incest.

If we understood the dire consequences of our actions, the severe damage they produce, we would walk much more gently before our God and our children. God knows the long-term, and in some cases permanent, damage that abuse produces in the victims' personalities and thought processes. He is also well aware of how open to spiritual oppression this particular sin leaves both victims and abusers. Under the Old Covenant, God's only cure for both victims and abusers was death. There was no blood yet shed holy or powerful enough to bring deliverance. If we only understood the level of change that occurs in the spirit, mind, will, and emotions of victims, in response to life situations and to people, we would better understand the judgment of God that we view as so harsh. We can all praise God for His great provision of deliverance through Jesus Christ. Under the New Covenant neither the victims nor their abusers are sentenced to death. After understanding how seriously God views this sin, we should have more compassion for the victims, and be willing to address their needs for deliverance and healing. As ministers and leaders, we must also become more committed to doing all we can to help the abusers to cease their actions and to receive the help they need to end the problem.

You can best describe personalities of sexual victims with one word—ambivalent. Working with them can be most frustrating, unless you recognize the symptoms and the spirits in operation. As their partners, mates, friends, or bosses, you begin to believe that you are crazy, or that they have a vendetta against you to drive you to distraction. As their pastors or spiritual leaders, you do not understand the battles and spiritual hindrances the victims seem to deliberately face, keeping themselves behind the proverbial 8-ball! They seem always to sin at the same point in their walk, just as success is in sight, or just as God is ready to move mightily on their behalf. This produces such frustration in you that you want to just give up on them and send them on their way to "bless" some other ministry.

For the sake of order, let us begin to break down some of the major areas of problems in the victim personality. We will then attempt at the conclusion to expose the spiritual principles operating in each of these areas.

PROBLEM AREAS.

A. Fear. Sexual victims are unaware of the origins of the many fears which so adversely inhibit their development and suppress their achievements. Their most common and universally expressed fears are:

1. Fear of being successful. Whether or not the victims are aware of this fear, its effects remain. As the individual is about to succeed, he will intentionally, albeit unconsciously, do something to turn the ship around, and end up being a complete failure, or partially successful at best. He will express frustration in never quite "making it," but he will have no idea what blocks his success. As difficult as it is for you to understand that their actions are not consciously planned, their lack of success is even more difficult for them to understand. They are shocked and frustrated and feel as though God doesn't want them to succeed. Some victims believe that only fate decrees success or lack of it. Some will say that there are those destined from birth for success and those destined to fail. Others will say that they believe they live under a curse, and still others are convinced that God has secret knowledge that renders them untrustworthy, or too evil to deserve success. However they express such beliefs, understand that they feel totally out of control of the situation, which adds to their feelings of helplessness.

2. Fear of failure. This fear always accompanies the fear of success. It creates the same wear and tear on its victims that is put on a car when both the accelerator and brake pedal are depressed simultaneously. The victims are driven to constant striving, trying to prove that they were NOT born evil. They will work harder,

for longer hours, will be more prone to take all the blame, and will still constantly wonder what is wrong with them. They will be more prone to investigate alternative ways to accomplish given tasks, so sure that their big break is inevitable if only they could find the right combination. They are as afraid of failure as they are of success, because they are looking for something to break the negative feelings they have about themselves, and also assume others to have.

3. Fear of God or any authority figure. These victims are convinced that God will do nothing but torture them or deny them the very things that they want. They are expecting to be as violated, misused, and hurt by God as they were by the abuser or abusers. Every victim of sexual abuse with whom we have worked has had a more difficult time with God than those who have not suffered this type of abuse. Even though they may have no memory of sexual abuse, they seem to be instinctively suspicious of God, as if they hold Him accountable for their circumstances that just never seem to go right.

4. Fear of taking leadership. Like victims of other types of abuse, they will not accept leadership roles unless forced into them. Unlike the others, they will more quickly find someone through whom they can feed their ideas and let that person achieve notoriety. This type of victim does have some idea of his innate abilities and talents. He really does desire to bring his dreams and ideas to successful conclusions, even though he is incapable of accomplishing it. So his new "star in the constellation" will be someone who enjoys an up-front position, but may have neither the creative ability to initiate new programs nor the wherewithal to carry them out on his own. Therefore the victim is able to vicariously and safely fulfill his natural gifts from behind the scenes. Warning: If this relationship continues, it will be as unhealthy for the front man as for the victim.

The main driving forces inside sexual victims that keep them from leadership (other than fear of success) are strong feelings of inferiority and feelings of innate worthlessness. They fear that if they were put into the stress of a leadership position where their true abilities and worth would be exposed, they would come up like a Hollywood set—merely a facade, having no real depth. Some confess to fears that if their true personalities were exposed, they would be compared to a shooting star, rather than a long-distance runner. There is a general mistrust of themselves, and a fear that if they accepted leadership roles, some deeply hidden part of themselves would be exposed, and they would be disgraced.

5. Fear of losing control. They are afraid that if they became emotional they would put themselves in danger of being harmed. They like to be in control of their environment. They try to have enough knowledge on a variety of topics to direct the flow of conversation around them, preventing its centering on them or exposing them. They will further take control of situations by the use of body language that loudly shouts, "You are too close, back off," or says, "I will not be involved in this action in any way." If worst comes to worst, they will try to intimidate everyone involved, or convince them that they are not worthy of the attention. This fear greatly affects their relationship with God. They limit what they allow themselves to experience, or what they allow God to do in their lives, especially in public. They also tend to deny the depth of their private relationship with God. Seldom indeed will victim personalities allow themselves public emotional encounters with God. They are not going to start shouting praises, running around the church, or freely operating in any of the gifts. They will not be found singing a solo, teaching a large group, or allowing themselves to be slain in the Spirit.

6. Fear of the dark and going to bed. Sexual victims become nervous at night and do not like going alone at night to an empty house or building. They tend to delay going to bed until LATE. You may well receive more calls

from these victims at night, because it seems that situations they have coped well with all day suddenly become more severe and beyond their coping strengths at night. They are using more effort just to cope with the darkness, even though they do not realize it.

7. Fear of violence or pain. They will do anything to avoid both—except during those periods when they feel a need for punishment. These victims are afraid that at any given moment someone will inflict upon them the pain and violation of rape, physical abuse, or physical harm of some type. This fear stems from the fact that the original abuse primarily occurred for no rhyme or reason. Most victims feel that since they did nothing to deserve the initial violation, the pattern will continue for the rest of their lives, resulting in their being completely unable to trust God OR man.

8. Fear of those resembling their abuser. These victims will seem to worship their abusers, and to highly respect their opinions. However, they will show obvious fear of people who are of the same sex and general build as their original abusers. This is, of course, unconscious.

B. Mistrust of people. Victims expect most people to abuse them, to cause them emotional or physical pain. Some believe that people only associate with them for what they can produce or provide. Victims usually are good at sizing up people around them, and can give some good advice based on suspected motives. But in their own lives, they seem to keep at least one abuser around. Their discernment seems not to work on their own behalf. They can and do recognize and eliminate some personality types who would cause them difficulty, but their warning system is not effective in totally eliminating those who would destroy or discredit them. Victims usually tend to form love-hate relationships with their abusers, always working to gain their continuing approval and respect.

C. Lack of feelings and emotions. This symptom appears more often in those who were also physically or psychologically abused. It usually occurs in those who were only sexually abused IF they used their imaginations as defense mechanisms to escape the abuse. The lack of apparent emotion gives the victims an appearance of being cool, easygoing, unflappable, patient, and capable of handling situations and people that the average person would not tolerate. Part of their ability to live this way is their lack of emotion and feeling, but much of it is that they do not feel worthy of any better treatment. The victim himself will often realize the deadness he feels inside but is too afraid to ask for help. That would expose his secret fear that something is seriously wrong with him and that he needs to be put away. If they can feel anything at all, more often than not it will be anger, hurt, and fear. It is the positive emotions that are usually beyond their comprehension. Much pushing and much pressure must take place before they have any sensation of emotion. Most in this category of abuse have no understanding of love or what it means. That is a shocking statement, but the damage done by the abuser has not been fully appreciated by normal souls. This lack alone makes a true emotional commitment almost impossible to fulfill successfully. This also prevents a total commitment to God; it is as though they always hold some of themselves back, just out of His reach.

D. Language patterns. Victims seem always to apologize for everything. If you are around them much at all, you may think they are apologizing for being alive and taking up space. Their communication is centered around a pattern of continuous acquiescence. They will repeatedly give in and step back until they can no longer tolerate their pattern of retreat. Then you will observe some spunk until a little ground has been regained; unfortunately the cycle will start all over again. Overall, they will tend to be the peacemaker, whether they are directly involved in the disagreement or not. And they seem to instinctively know what to say to avoid a confrontation.

They will explain away anything they own that has the appearance of being above the poverty level, because they feel totally unworthy of any luxury. Upon receiving a compliment about something they are wearing, or something they own, they will tell you how old it is or identify it as a gift. They will NEVER be heard to say that they bought themselves a luxury item; they seem to feel so unclean and unworthy as to have no right to luxury. Accepting gifts is so difficult that, even if forced to receive them, they find it almost impossible to enjoy the bounty.

E. Expectations. They always expect the worst. It seems that sexual victims are the second type of people who blossom under adversity (the first being those addicted to adrenalin). Their theory of life seems to be that IF something good happens it will be followed by something BAD, so why allow the good? Please note that this, more than any other characteristic, ruins their spiritual life. It is as though they stand before God with their hands closed, refusing His blessings. Their view of God is thus distorted, because they believe that God's promises work for everyone but them.

F. Amnesia. This breaks down into four categories depending on the severity of the problem and the coping mechanism the victims used:

1. Total. The victims have very little memory of childhood, which leads to frustration and fear. First, they believe they have no past to serve as a foundation on which to build the present and future. Even worse is a nagging fear that there is something so terrible in their past that, were it ever exposed, it would utterly destroy them.

2. Selective. This group remembers only the good events that happened. Believe it or not, from our observations this causes more emotional problems than the preceding category. While growing up, the victims formed a false adulation of their family members, always

making themselves the villains in any problem. Therefore, they now feel guilty for their unexplained negative feelings.

3. Partial. These victims have a mixture of both good and bad memories of the past. At least the bad memories are non-threatening. Of the four types, this victim is the most difficult to work with. He believes that since his memory is so good, there could not be anything else back there, no matter how many symptoms plague his life. In this category are the unique individuals who may remember one or two instances of abuse (of any of the three types), but their memories will protect them from remembering the abusers who are the most threatening. The victims may have created a relationship with their abusers based on such fantasy that their very sanity would be threatened should this relationship be broken. Their memories may well be protecting them from both the perpetrators and the initial acts, as well as the frequency of attacks.

4. Fantasy. These individuals have created memories that are 90% to 95% false. There is just enough truth to pass inspection and give them an identity, but it creates conversations and positive relationships with family members that never existed. This therefore intensifies the guilt felt about admitting that anything less than total love could have transpired within their families. It also places them in positions of continually striving to earn the love and approval of their families.

This problem of amnesia in any of the above categories affects other areas of the individual's life. He may have a problem retaining information learned in school. This may cause him to feel that his I.Q. is far below what it actually is, or that he must have a learning disability. He may also have problems with short-term memory, appearing to others as though he never listens or pays attention. None of these is actually true at all.

In all four categories there are periods when the victim knows (even though unconsciously) that some event back there in his past was a painful experience. This may manifest itself in a variety of ways:

a. A dream in which the figures are slightly shapeless, unidentifiable and disjointed.

b. A vague fear that someone is hiding under his bed.

c. A fleeting impression that a form is standing in the doorway—and panic is the result.

These may occur in dreams, as well as at times of complete consciousness, but fear almost always accompanies these events and there is terror at the thought of remembering their cause. Even though there is no memory of the abuse, he finds it difficult, if not impossile, to watch a TV show or read any material on the subject of abuse.

G. How they view themselves. They always feel inferior to everyone else. They work overtime at being accepted, liked, and valued. However, since they do not see themselves in this light, it is the same deception as a victim of anorexia looking in the mirror and seeing a fat person. It is impossible to infuse any reality into their perception of themselves. They try in many ways to earn love and respect but will never be able to accept it, thereby frustrating everyone close to them. They express these feelings either by communicating an attitude that "everything's cool," or by trying to act as if they are in complete control. Another defense mechanism used is their need to know something about everything. Either that or they tend to suffer from inertia, both to avoid judgment or exposure. Sexual victims are prone to self-destructive behavior. They usually hate themselves: who they are, what they are, and what they do.

H. Relationships. Sexual victims MUST have an abuser around somewhere. If they cannot find an abuser or force someone into that role, they will abuse themselves. They will use overwork, denial of pleasure, goals set just out of reach, self-denial of something they want or would enjoy, or will place themselves in positions of receiving pain. Be warned: they know how to turn a normal person into a temporary abuser.

I. Sexual attitudes. In this area we seem to find the greatest variety of reactions. Some victims believe that everything that occurred was their fault, that they were sirens and tempted the abuser into the act. If they have no memory, they feel like they cannot be trusted. They think that at every opportunity they will lure the opposite sex into a relationship, so they do everything possible to avoid all contact.

Their sex lives will break down into one of the following expressions:

1. They will not engage in ANY sex because they believe that sex is dirty.

2. They will find the marriage relationship almost impossible. They feel that sex is a "service" and not a means of intimate communication. (Remember that both sexes can be involved in the giving and receiving of service.) If someone in this category does marry, the marriage is likely to run into serious trouble or even break up over sexual and affection problems.

3. They will have big problems giving and receiving affection. They may seem to be frigid, but the truth is that they are uncomfortable with and afraid of warmth and intimacy.

4. They may have a low sex drive even if married. If the victim is the male, he will tend to vent his repressed feelings of rage and indignation. The sex act will be more like rape than love. If the victim is female, she will tend to be passive and completely uninvolved, almost as though she is planning her day or writing her grocery list. This appears to stem from the fact that as a child her means of coping was to just "not be there." In marriage she will not usually initiate the sex act, as she has a fear

of the penis. As another alternative, she will sometimes become tense and uncommunicative.

5. If the victim is a male, he may tend toward perversion, kinky sex, varied positions, or may advance to sado-masochism under the guise of boredom.

6. The male victim MAY tend more to masturbation, while the female MAY have a problem even touching her own body.

7. The victims, either male or female, may become so sexually active that they run the risk of severe promiscuity, which borders on prostitution.

8. Responses 5, 6 and 7 lead to constant experimentation with position, with partner, and with different acts. It can also lead to the need for pain and humiliation, or even group involvement.

9. When homosexuality and lesbianism are the resulting sexual patterns, the victims were usually sodomized.

J. Damage to parenting ability. Some of the abused parents will instill in their children a sense of mistrust or fear of close family members, without realizing what they are doing or why. Some will fight urges toward incestual relationships with their own children, or will molest other children. Fortunately, most will be able to confine such urges to fantasy.

As can clearly be observed by the preceding paragraphs, sexual abuse leaves no area of its victims' lives intact. The influence of the abusers is stamped deep into the nature and personalities of his victims. Is it any wonder that before Jesus came the only way to effectively treat the problem was death?

In II Samuel 13:1-20 we find a record of incest. The account records responses of both the victim and the abuser. Amnon loved Tamar, so he tricked her into his room, then raped her. In verse 15 we read:

Then Amnon hated her exceedingly; so that the

*hatred wherewith he hated her was greater than the
love wherewith he had loved her. . . . "*

His response to that new feeling of hatred was to throw
her out and lock her out. Whether or not most abusers
intend it, their sexual actions are interpreted by their
victims as hatred and contempt.

In verses 12-13, 16, 19-20, Tamar's feelings and reactions
are recorded, and the damage done to her emotions. In
verse 12 Tamar delineated the following feelings and
reactions:

1. Please do not force me: Victims, if they could
express anything to their abusers, would make it
plain that they were being forced to do something
that violates their very innermost being.

2. Do not humble me: All victims will readily admit
that the strongest feelings are those of humiliation
and defilement.

3. Do not disgrace me: In verse 13, Tamar became
even more expressive and asked, "How could I ever
rid myself of this shame?"

When dealing with victims of sexual abuse of any type,
be aware that they all believe that they can never be freed
from the shame and guilt. These victims believe that they
must always feel dirty inside, unclean, evil, and unworthy.
In verse 16 Tamar begged, "Do not send me away, because
that is worse than the act." Most victims will admit that
the most devastating realization is that they were merely
throw-away toys, to be played with and then discarded.
They find it difficult to accept as fact that the motivation
for such acts was not love, even though it would be
perverted love, but was indeed lust, hatred, or contempt.
Most abusers want the victims out of their lives as soon as
they no longer are of any use or pleasure.

In verse 19 Tamar expressed and acted out her reactions.
She mourned. Every victim seems to feel deep sorrow,
even grief, that she can neither shake nor explain. She felt
as if something had died. We suggest that it is more than

the death of her innocence and virginity. Most victims state that their emotions died. At some point during the violation, their sense of self-respect and even their identity as an individual died. Tamar cried uncontrollably. When a victim comes to realize the abuse that has occurred, it is not uncommon for the response to be uncontrolled crying. Such crying MAY occur at a later stage of recovery.

In verse 20 a description of Tamar's future is recorded and it describes the life of every victim—before and until deliverance.

"So Tamar remained desolate in her brother Absalom's house."

When ministering to sexually abused victims you will ALWAYS have to break the spirit and power of the abuser over the victim. You may find some of the following as well:

1. Fear of the attack and attacker.
2. Fear of pain and violence.
3. Fear of exposure.
4. Fear of memory and amnesia.
5. Fear of the night, fear of the bed.
6. Fear of failure.
7. Fear of success, and of leadership.
8. Fear of emotions and feelings.
9. Fear of people.
10. Fear of God and authority figures.
11. Fear of losing control.
12. Fear of sex.
13. Fear of people of the same sex as the attacker.
14. Fear of intimacy and closeness.
15. Unclean spirits.
16. Spirits of unworthiness *cause* feelings of unworthiness.
17. Worthless.
18. Shame, humiliation, guilt.
19. Mourning, grief, sorrow, weeping.
20. Poverty, and fear of poverty.

21. Any and all others pertinent to the victim with whom you are dealing.

Remember to always pray that God heal the memories and emotions of the person. Be forewarned that it is quite unlikely that God will deal completely with all these areas the very first time that you minister. Remember that you are asking God to restore a complete personality to wholeness. It will take time, much time, for that healing, and much love during the process.

The victims may also go through some of the following experiences, and they are NORMAL. We have seen them occur to varying degrees with each victim with whom we have dealt.

1. They will walk into their closet one day and realize that NOTHING is really them, so they will start all over trying to decide what IS the real "them."
2. They may suddenly re-do their entire home, room by room, for the same reason. Some former victims have even enlarged their homes.
3. Their taste in food may completely change. Some have been addicted to chocolate and sugar and now find their taste for them almost gone.
4. Their taste in friends will change as will their choices of whom they will date.

This is a confusing and somewhat frightening time for these former victims. Be patient, be prepared to walk with them as they discover who they really are and what it is they really can do! Be prepared for this, however. They will have an almost uncontrollable urge to tell SOMEONE about their past, to test their acceptance. It will usually be the most dangerous person they know, the most likely to judge them or to abuse the information. Caution them NOT to share their healing just yet. Also caution your former victims that thought patterns are also habits, and will take time to break. Just as a smoker will reach for his cigarettes for some days after he has quit, so will the former thought habits arise. Be prepared to pray with him and stand with him until he is able to walk alone.

THE EVENTUAL CHANGE WITHIN THE PERSON-ALITY WILL BE SO GREAT THAT WHEN THE HEALING PROCESS IS COMPLETE, THOSE CLOSEST TO THESE FORMER VICTIMS FEEL LIKE THEY HAVE MET A DIFFERENT PERSON.

Chapter 10

PHYSICAL ABUSE

In this chapter you will see many of the same symptoms and traits that appeared in the preceding chapter. We honestly feel that, because there are such strong connections in the spiritual realm between the body, soul and spirit, what affects the body introduces problems into both the soul (mind, will, and emotions) and spirit of the individual involved. Therefore it comes as no surprise to us that someone who has been battered and beaten will end up in need of ministry both to the soul and the spirit.

Some of the same areas will be involved as in cases of sexual molestation, even though that type of abuse affects primarily the soul. As in the preceding chapter, please realize that not every victim will display all of the symptoms or traits. It will depend upon the intensity of the physical abuse, the frequency of abuse, length of time spent being abused and the individual's own responses to the abuse and to the abuser. In another chapter we will discuss people who have been abused by their mates. You will be surprised at the many areas of similarity, as well as the areas of difference.

Listed below are the physical symptoms of victims of physical abuse. Many will be extremely familiar:

A. Clothing. Very dark, unflattering, unstylish and inappropriate for the occasion. Their outfits simply do not blend together as well as they should. Their unfashionable mode of dress can more adequately be described as Early Thrift Store, no matter how much it cost. The best description for this group is that their overall appearance makes a statement of never having been instructed in the fine art of dressing, or that they just do not care and cannot be bothered. They seem to grab the nearest articles of clothing and put them on, even though they may need washing. Their clothing also conveys an attitude of poverty, and says, "I am not worth anything."

B. Hair. Their hair will appear unkempt, dirty and oily and poorly styled. Whereas the sexually abused will try to hide behind their hair, a physically abused person seems to be trying to convey the message "I am not here" or "Please forget you saw me."

C. Appearance. Once again you observe what some have described as a gray pallor, actually an indescribable cast to the complexion that you learn to recognize. The physically abused do nothing to enhance their natural appearance, even tending to be quite carelessly put-together. The subconscious message they are sending is, "You won't approve of me anyway, neither are you going to like me, because no one else does." They will be ultra-conservative in the use of make-up, accessories and after-shave or colognes. They will do nothing to their persons that will call attention to themselves in any way at all. This is the person about whom your children would say, "Boy, what a nerd!" You might even find yourself thinking that they look like losers. In most cases that is far from the truth. Like sexually abused individuals, they have lived their entire lives in their minds. Therefore they have developed intricate patterns of deduction and evaluation, and their minds are by now extremely sharp!

D. Physical environment. Their homes are usually extremely cluttered and may even look as if a large windstorm just passed through. One of the victims we have observed expressed it best: "It seems that I clean it up and overnight someone slips in and dumps their clutter and dirt in my house." It is not that most victims are lazy, it is that their minds and spirits are so cluttered that the clutter expresses itself in the physical environment. In addition, they feel so bad about themselves that they do not have the energy or motivation to keep their environments different from the way they keep themselves.

E. Sleep habits. They have a propensity to violent nightmares but will usually wake up before the action has run its course. The characters in their dreams will be barely distinguishable if they have any memory of their own abuse. With or without memory, they will usually be a victim even in their dreams. The one major exception is that if their memory is intact, then in the beginning of their dreams the roles may be reversed so that they are the abusers. They also will need to sleep facing the door, usually with a small light on. They are prone to very poor sleep habits.

They may not remember dreaming when they awaken but those sleeping nearby will be aware of their restless sleep. They may toss and turn a lot, they may mutter, cry out or even talk in their sleep. When questioned while they are in a semi-sleep state they will describe a dream of being chased or hunted down or captured and mistreated by someone. By the next morning, however, they will have no memory of the dream at all, or only a knowledge that they did dream something. They will also experience the death-like sleep of a sexual victim and will also wake up more tired than when they went to bed. Also, similar to the sexual victim, they are instantly wide awake if someone crosses the threshold of their room. Their memory is usually better than that of a sexual victim, but they have just as hard a time connecting the past abuse with their present sleep habits because they find it difficult to lay any blame on their abusers.

F. Body language. These victims nonverbally communicate pent-up rage without even realizing it. As the observer you may translate it as coldness, arrogance, or overconfidence. Also, they are easily threatened and intimidated by what they perceive as a show of force. Without even realizing it, a counselor may speak loudly, confidently or with an authoritarian approach, and this victim hears him as shouting, or worse yet as arguing. Most victims of physical abuse will express in some form or other, "I will do anything, just do not shout or cry!"

Furthermore these victims require a wide territorial space, and become extremely uncomfortable when their comfort zone is invaded. If threatened, they will shift their position to reestablish the security of that zone, if necessary going to great lengths to do so. They are always alert to movement in their peripheral vision, and take instant action to protect themselves if they interpret any movement as one that could strike their body. If they hear an unidentifiable noise which sounds like a door slamming, or something being thrown or falling, they tend to make a reflex jerk or jump, and ask nervously, "What was that?" They usually feel so stupid and embarrassed afterward that they try to explain away their fear. You will also notice that they have very rapid eye movements and are constantly checking their immediate environment for danger, even for new people coming on the scene.

They will NEVER sit or stand in any way that puts their back to the door or crowd. They also will not permit themselves to be hemmed into a corner, or into the center of the crowd. They are terrified if touched or hugged from the back, particularly if they did not expect the contact. Their body will instantly stiffen, they will gasp, or give a little cry of surprise or will try to wriggle free enough to get a glimpse of their assailant. Some will do all of the above so quickly it seems super-human in speed. They prefer to initiate all intimate or affectionate encounters themselves.

The psychological description of this type of victim will follow. Once again, it must be pointed out that we are dealing with persons who behave as they do because of what they have experienced at the hands of someone they should have been able to trust.

God created families to illustrate His love for humanity, even His care for our bodies. For many years Satan has been trying to destroy this institution for two very good reasons. First, he realizes that if he can destroy the life of the family and bring in violence and violation, he can severely hamper the victims' abilities to relate, trust and obey God out of love and not fear. If he can create enough victims who mistrust God as much as they do people, and attribute the same evil motives to God they do to people, he will have severely handicapped the church. He will be much more free to accomplish his own goals for mankind. Second, he will try to destroy the only pattern we have for understanding our relationship with God, and also that His intentions for us are ALWAYS good. When we understand this concept there will be nothing we will not do for God at His request. In Jeremiah 29:11 God reassured His people this way:

> *For I know the thoughts that I think toward you, saith the LORD, thoughts of peace, and not of evil, to give you an expected end."*

The best description of the physically abused individual is: guarded, fearful, and full of latent rage ready to explode like a volcano with no warning or plan. As a leader or pastor, these people can be your greatest asset or your most time-consuming liability.

Now let us begin to dissect some of the major problem areas in the personalities of these victims, and we will attempt at the conclusion to expose the spiritual forces in operation in each area.

A. Fear. The victim of physical abuse is controlled by as many fears as the sexual victim, but the expression of them is different as is the behavior they produce. You will recognize many that appear below and perhaps a better understanding of the connection between the body, soul and spirit will result.

1. Fear of being successful. As in the case of sexual victims, these people are unaware that they are blocking success in their lives. They usually sabotage their own efforts just as success is within reach. They do not

realize that they are their own worst enemies. They find it difficult to understand that they are largely to blame, since they work so hard to achieve their goals. Most of them say that it's either GOD'S fault, or some unknown force or curse they were born under.

2. Fear of failure. This fear always accompanies the one above. Here also there is emotional wear and tear, and increased emotional pressure such as most of us cannot imagine. They are so afraid of failure because each failure reinforces every negative thought and feeling they have ever had about themselves.

3. Fear of receiving notoriety or recognition. If it becomes apparent that this victim is to be honored for a job well done, that his natural talent or ability has been refined to the point of public recognition, or that something he has created is deemed valuable enough for exposure to an audience, he will panic. He will go to great lengths to bring to a halt any and all public exposure of ANY of his accomplishments. This is caused by an unconscious fear that once held up for public view he will not be accepted or deemed valuable enough for others to admire.

4. Fear of taking leadership. Like the other two types of victims, he will not assume leadership roles unless forced into them. This individual has even less of a concept than does the sexual victim that something of worth is inside him somewhere. He becomes an AMBIV-ALENT LEADER, which means that as the group or responsibility grows it appears headless. He will find making decisions almost impossible. He will try to find the consensus of opinion thereby making the group rule itself, or wait and let things just happen. This leaves the group sensing that they have no real direction and are just drifting along. This causes rebellion to occur, either overt or covert, with strong personalities taking control, by suggestions that they make or directions they give.

5. Fear of God or any authority figure. Since they are accustomed to an authority figure abusing them, they naturally assume that anyone in authority over them will

misuse and abuse them. They are even more afraid of God than the other two types of victims since they are well aware of the judgment side of His nature. They believe that they have always been so "bad" as to DESERVE repeated punishment, having always been told that they brought their punishment on themselves. They naturally assume that God feels the same way about them. Some even believe He knew they were evil and that is why life has been such an awful experience for them.

6. Fear of losing control. They fear that the result of losing control of their emotions or their environment would only be further hurt. Since most believe that they have protected themselves from further hurt by out-thinking and out-reacting their abuser, most of these victims NEVER RELAX. They are continually evaluating everyone in their environment, which makes it difficult for people to attempt any close relationship with them. It makes others feel put off, mistrusted or disliked. Therefore, people stop trying to be friends with these victims. This adds to their problems as they begin to feel lonely and even more unworthy. They tend to control all conversations so that talk flows around them, but never gets close enough for them to be made transparent. You will NEVER see victims of this type allowing a public encounter with God which would result in the slightest loss of control. In fact, the best description for this person is stoic. Even in a church setting they will attempt to avoid taking an up-front position where they would be required to become transparent.

7. Fear of crowds. These victims are often afraid of speaking before groups. They fear that everything bad or lacking in them will be seen by everyone present. They would lose whatever respect and whatever friendships they do have. They avoid being put into any situation requiring them to be evaluated, exposed or criticized.

8. Fear of criticism. This always exists with the preceding fear. It is more pronounced in the psychological

victim than here, but it still has to be dealt with. They are so fragile, and their own concept of themselves so shaky, that any negative statement by someone they love or value can do irreparable damage to their emotional make-up.

9. Fear of the dark and of going to bed. These individuals will start becoming nervous as night approaches. They will tend not to cope with problems as well at night as during the day, and will call for help more often at night. They do NOT like going into an empty building at night. They are extremely nervous about being left alone at night. They are prone to feel that something evil or harmful will surface. It is almost as though the old bogeyman existed after all!

10. Fear of violence or pain. They will do ANYTHING to avoid both *EXCEPT* when they feel the need for punishment. These victims will always have an abuser in their environment ready to inflict the pain they need. However, since these victims mistrust everyone, they expect abuse on a regular basis whether they feel the need or not.

B. Mistrust of people. The victims feel that there is nothing within them valuable enough to merit approval, so they never expect good interactions with anyone. They naturally assume that if they do something well, someone else will come in and take the glory away from them. Once again, these victims are exceptional at sizing up those around everyone but themselves. They are prone to have great discernment about the motives of other people. Be careful lest you mistake this for critical judgment.

C. Lack of feelings and emotions. These victims cannot control their reactions, nor seem to find a way to activate their feelings and emotions. They have used their intellect as a defense mechanism of self-protection. These victims seem to be aloof, cool, arrogant, unflappable and patient. They seem to be able to work with people and in situations others find almost impossible. This ability stems from their own feelings of such worthlessness, uselessness and inadequacy that they dare not judge others lest their own weaknesses become more noticeable. These victims have so much latent rage, anger, resentment and hatred that they can feel these emotions, if no others. However, because they realize how easy it would be for them to lose control, they work hard at repression. Many become so exhausted they get less done than they should, or they suffer from unusually violent dreams.

D. Language patterns. They apologize for everything. They seem to feel responsible for everything that does not run smoothly. Their speech patterns are also centered around a pattern of continual subservience. They continue to step back further until they are pushed beyond their tolerance, then they fight to regain some of the ground they have lost. Overall they are peacemakers in every situation and with all people. They have a poverty-level vocabulary and cannot easily deal with abundance or praise. They will continually explain away anything they own as either old or a gift. They will talk down any compliment they receive and even embarrass the person giving the compliment. They will not buy for themselves anything they cannot justify as a valuable contribution for their work, or for making a situation easier to deal with. They will always try to find someone else or something else that will benefit as much if not more from their purchase.

E. Expectations. They always expect the worst! They believe themselves only capable of producing inferior work, therefore nothing good *should* result. They expect to work and work and never receive any reward or benefit from their labors. They never have in the past. (They do not understand that they have placed that limit on themselves. They would deny any and all responsibility for such a problem.) These people also seem to blossom under pressure and usually are very proud of that. This distorts their ability to receive blessings from God, as well as to see Him as a loving Father.

F. Amnesia. This group of victims does not seem to have

severe problems with amnesia as do sexual victims, UNLESS the abuse has almost resulted in their death, in a permanent handicap, or in scars to their bodies. If their memories are affected, it will most likely center around the frequency of the abuse, its intensity or the primary abuser. Most victims in this group will say that you "just do not understand" how difficult they were to raise. They believe that this excuses the actions of the abuser and places the blame where they feel it should rest—on themselves. If there IS any tendency at all to amnesia, you may observe one of the following patterns:

1. A problem with retention will make them seem to have a lower I.Q. than they do, or will be mistaken as a learning disability.

2. They will have a problem with short-term memory making them appear not to listen or pay attention to people.

Added to their seeming arrogance, these problems could convince one that they are selfish and self-centered. This could not be further from the truth and usually adds to their problems of always feeling unloved and misjudged.

G. How they view themselves.

1. They continually feel inferior to everyone. They overwork at being loved, accepted and viewed as having some self-worth. But since they cannot accept these attitudes about themselves, they can never receive them from someone else. They need constant reinforcement and reassurance that they are doing a good job, or are good people, but they will never receive such as truth. Therefore they are the most frustrating people to befriend or to work with.

2. They are so full of self-hatred that they hate WHO they are, WHAT they are, and EVERYTHING THEY DO! Nor can they trust themselves. They are afraid that if they ever did lose control, they would become extremely violent.

3. They are afraid to share their inner feelings, their inner selves, with ANYONE!

4. They tend to self-destruct.

H. They will have an abuser in their environment at all times. This group will tend to date abusers, even marry abusers. They may well have a boss or someone they work with who is an abuser. If they cannot find an abuser, or make someone in their environment into an abuser, they will then suffer abuse somehow, even if it is only to deprive themselves of a want or need. They will also be prone to put themselves into painful situations.

J. They will maintain a protected position whatever their stance. They will usually appear frightened, shy, and easily intimidated.

K. They will be very prone to abusing their spouses (who were probably victims themselves before marriage) or their children.

L. They will NEVER (prior to receiving ministry) be the person who should work in day-care centers or in nursing homes. They will have a propensity to abuse individuals in their environment who cause them frustration.

M. They have a great deal of difficulty in giving on an emotional level to those who are important to them. They then overcompensate by giving too much to those who do not mean nearly so much!

N. They will always form a love-hate relationship with their abusers. They will defend them to everyone, and will allow no one to attack the abusers or their character in any way. And yet they are terrified of the abusers and at times fight violent urges to kill them, or maim or harm them in some lasting and visible manner.

O. They will work throughout their entire lives, even long after the abuser is dead, to gain the abuser's approval. They believe unconsciously that if the abuser ever approved of them they would be valid and worthwhile human beings.

As can be observed from the preceding paragraphs, physical abuse harms more than just the body. It leaves bruises on the mind, will, emotions and spirit of the victim. These wounds often form scars that remain sensitive to pressure and often break open at the most inopportune moments. Is it any wonder that when Jesus chose a section to read that would best illustrate the purposes of His ministry, He read from Isaiah 61:1-3? We find this recorded in Luke 4:18-19:

The Spirit of the Lord is upon me, because He hath anointed Me to preach the gospel to the poor; He hath sent Me to heal the brokenhearted, to preach deliverance to the captives and recovering of sight to the blind, to set at liberty them that are bruised, to preach the acceptable year of the Lord.

In Matthew 12:20 we find this further description of the Messiah's ministry:

A bruised reed shall He not break, and smoking flax shall He not quench, till He send forth judgment unto victory.

The word "reed" apparently refers to a musical instrument which shepherds used to soothe the sheep, and also used to worship the Lord. This reed pipe was so fragile that if it did break, the shepherd would devote hours to repairing it rather than to crush it underfoot and start over. Just so are we in the hands of our Creator, Who is our Shepherd. We are so fragile, so easily broken and bruised. And yet in the right hands, with the proper care, our lives can be used to comfort, encourage and soothe other sheep. He, like that earthly shepherd, will spend countless hours with us, gently repairing us, rather than discarding us to start over. He often uses people to repair people, by His power and the use of His gifts.

When ministering to these victims, you must always break the spirit and power of their abusers over them. This only represents an evil spirit that has taken up an assignment against them (see II Pet. 2:19b). You will find some of the following as well:

A. Fear of the attack and attacker.
B. Fear of pain and violence.
C. Fear of exposure.
D. Fear of remembering, and amnesia.
E. Fear of the night, and fear of being alone.
F. Fear of success and of leadership
   (perhaps a fear of successful leadership also).
G. Fear of failure (yes, there can be both of these).
H. Fear of notoriety and public achievement.
I. Fear of crowds and fear of people.
J. Fear of emotions and feelings.
K. Fear of God and authority figures.
L. Fear of losing control.
M. Fear of intimacy and close relationships.
N. Fear of being physically touched.
O. Unclean spirit.
P. Unworthy, unloved, hurt and wounded spirits.
Q. Worthlessness and uselessness.
R. Poverty and fear of poverty.
S. Rage, anger, hate, and self-hate.
T. Violence, murder, and abuse.
U. All other spirits pertaining to the victim with whom you are working.

Remember to pray always that God heal the memories *and* emotions of the victim. Be aware that with these victims (as well as with the other types) it is unlikely during their first time of ministry that God will expose every area that needs attention. They simply would not be able to stand in all those areas at once (see Deut. 7:22-23). Remember to be patient; God is restoring a very fragile and much-damaged personality. They must become accustomed to being themselves. More than you can understand, they need room to experiment with the person they really are, time to learn what their talents and capabilities are, and their likes and dislikes. They may well be unsure of themselves, frightened and confused.

God seems to be saying through all the problems in the body of Christ today, "I make all things new," NOT "I make all new things!"

Whatever category they fall into, most victims are so bruised and so damaged that your job first and foremost will be to convince them that things CAN be different, and WILL be different. Not until after ministry will you be able to persuade most of them that they are basically "good," that they CAN succeed at life, that they may even have something good to contribute to the lives of others. Most of them cannot believe that they CAN be happy, that they DESERVE to be happy, that it is NOT WRONG to be happy, nor even to WISH for happiness! Certainly they never expected God to do anything good for THEM, only for everyone else. Ahead of you lies an extremely difficult task, but, in Christ Jesus,

IT CAN BE DONE!

Chapter 11

PSYCHOLOGICAL ABUSE

This chapter deals with the area of psychological abuse. There is neither a clear definition nor an absolute standard by which to determine the point at which verbal and nonverbal communication or environmental restrictions and demands become abusive. Thus, because of its nebulous nature, psychological abuse must be classified as the most insidious of all. Identification and treatment are further complicated and hindered for the following reasons:

I. We cannot define conclusively what may be detrimental to one's mind, to one's emotions, or to the formation of personality. Nor can we set definitively safe limits on the use of correction or discipline.

II. Psychological abuse neither violates nor penetrates the physical body, nor are there distinct marks on the victims, as with sexual abuse or physical abuse. Therefore, it leaves no physical signs to be detected medically.

III. All human beings have suffered psychological abuse to some degree at some time in their lives. Because of that, we are more inured to symptoms associated with this type of abuse. We tend to believe, and to tell its victims, "That is the way life is, get used to it."

While psychological abuse may not have definitive standards, it does yield results in the minds and emotions of its victims which can be seen and defined. Improbable though it may seem, victims of psychological abuse are often more damaged than victims of either physical or sexual abuse. Victims of psychological abuse have no moment to pinpoint as the specific time of their abuse. The physically or sexually abused can attribute their abuse and their resulting problems to the violence or lust of certain persons at specific times. Remember that neither physical nor sexual abuse can occur as often as psychological abuse.

Verbal abusers usually know how to accomplish their abuse in public, and do it so subtly that only their victims know what is going on. Should these victims react, knowing well the message behind the remarks, the abuser's tendency to abuse is reinforced. Those observing the exchange usually assume the victims to be the persons with the problem. Anyone observing such a public exchange would think the victims guilty of overreacting, being overly sensitive, unreasonable, or just plain mean and hard to live with. This is extremely damaging to the emotional welfare of the victims.

Most who abuse psychologically are also masters at subtly controlling the environment of their victims until only those of whom the abusers approve have free access to the victims. Abusers also tend to control the outside activities of the victims. This furthers the controlling power of the abusers over the lives of their victims. Abusers are fearful of their victims forming trusting relationships with authority figures lest the authority figure expose the abuser, and their victims break free!

The confusion in evaluating psychological abuse is compounded by the fact that abusers will sometimes also physically, and even sexually, abuse their victims. If this happens, it serves to convince the victims that their behavior caused so much stress and frustration that the abusers could not help the abuse. There are many psychological abusers who never adopt another form of abuse, but they are so verbally destructive when under great stress that the effect on their victims is the same as physical abuse.

To give some assistance in recognizing potentially abusive situations, we must understand that psychological abuse occurs not only in marriages, but between parents and their children, employers and employees, roommates and even friends. Victims will always form at least one abusive relationship. Victims cannot live without abusers, nor can abusers thrive without victims. If we broaden our ideas of the types of relationships this form of abuse can affect, some situations that might have escaped our attention may well come into focus.

For our purposes, then, the working definition for psychological abuse includes:

1. Any type of communication that is critical, humiliating and otherwise consistently destructive to the emotional security, self-image, self-worth, and development of another person.

2. Artificially imposed environmental controls that make one individual the psychological or physical prisoner of another.

3. The setting, by the abusers, of unrealistically high standards and goals, producing feelings of failure, inadequacy, self-hatred and shame in their victims.

Psychological abuse causes such deep wounds to the identity and self-worth of its victims that they are hindered in forming ANY healthy relationships. They perceive their self-worth to be under attack by anyone in a close relationship, even when there is no attack. They have a desperate need to feel valuable, but cannot specify any behavior that would achieve this important end. Victims know how they would like to be treated by other people, but at times have difficulty knowing how to translate that information into practical action. They are easily threatened and feel insecure because of their perception of how others view them and view the way they execute their jobs and responsibilities. They seldom feel indispensable, or appreciated, and always feel taken for granted. The victims usually believe (although unconsciously) that the world has a higher set of standards for them, allowing absolutely no room for mistakes or less-than-perfect performance. At this stage of development, victims feel thoroughly drained. They perceive everyone to be drawing from them, demanding answers, support and direction. Such feelings lead to either panic or depression, because victims do not believe that they have any of these resources available, even for themselves. They feel taken advantage of and taken for granted, and they often are.

Remember that the primary weapons of the abusers are intimidation and ridicule. This unique combination causes the victims to keep trying to perform and produce in a vain attempt to gain validation from their abusers. Sometimes the abusers use a third tactic and belittle their victims, attacking their gender or the core of their identity. This attack wounds so deeply that the victims question their very foundations, their concepts and values. If this wound is inflicted often enough, victims begin to experience such confusion that they feel unable to reach the simplest conclusions. They begin to question their most basic rights, concluding that these standards are also wrong. The abusers now have gained such a level of control that, with a little planning, they can even determine the kind of treatment their victims will expect to receive from others. For example, an abuser might say to his victim, "If you do that, so-and-so will see how dumb you are." His victim is by now so weakened that she accepts such statements as fact. In order not to appear "dumb," the victim retreats within herself and says nothing. It is even possible for the situation to deteriorate so much that the victims begin to look to their abusers for validation of their value systems, their choice of friends and their outside activities.

Some abusers will attack an area in which the victims already believe themselves handicapped or inferior. For example, if they are naturally awkward, their abusers will begin to taunt them about their lack of dexterity skills. This heightens their awkwardness, allowing the abusers more opportunity to make fun of them in public. If they have physical limitations, their abusers will repeatedly put them in situations which spotlight those sensitive areas. Cruel as this is, the most severe damage seems to occur when abusers attack areas of fear or insecurity within their victims, and make them a public laughing stock. This produces some of the same personality problems as being raped. Once this method is begun, no opportunity for such abuse is overlooked. The abusers enjoy public scenes that illustrate their point. They frequently turn conversations so that there is an opportunity to produce embarrassment, humiliation or force the victims to poke fun at themselves. Since these victims have now been programmed to sensitivity concerning these issues, they often GIVE the abuser an opening to attack. At least they still have enough control over their lives to determine when the abuse will occur, and they can get it over with. This unconscious thought process seems quite illogical, but it does serve to eliminate some of the helplessness these victims feel.

Psychological abuse leaves its victims in continual need of affirmation and reassurance, even when performing the simplest tasks. Pastors and counselors must beware of this. Without some understanding of abuse, these victims may seem to be conceited, wanting everyone to appreciate their performance. This could not be further from the truth. Victims truly need ego reinforcement. They think they always fail and never do anything right. These victims have no realistic idea of their value, accomplishments, appearance, or effect on others. They never see themselves as successful, competent, or valuable.

It is difficult to conceive of one individual so destroyed by another, but destruction is exactly the product of constant negative attacks. Try a simple experiment. Tell one person over and over that they seem to be tired. Before you know it, that person feels exhausted, whether or not they have reason.

How amazing is the power and truth of Proverbs 18:21:

Death and life are in the power of the tongue: and they that love it shall eat the fruit thereof.

The book of Exodus tells us that twelve spies were sent to look over Canaan. Ten of those spies reported how huge the giants were and how small the Israelites seemed, and, by their words, kept the entire nation from conquering their Land of Promise. The other two spies, Joshua and Caleb, were eager to obey God and take the land, but they were overruled. Not only did the ten spies eat the fruit of their own lips, but so did their three million or so victims. If we understood the power of the tongue to create or destroy, perhaps we would be more careful of what we spoke. Remember that in Hebrews 11:3, we are told that God SPOKE the world into existence.

Psychologically abused victims have virtually no confidence in their own talents or abilities. To produce true intense anxiety or even in some cases terror, ask them to perform. They always expect to be critically evaluated, and thereby exposed as failures and frauds. No matter how accomplished they may be, they never see their abilities in a positive light. They question love and respect, believing that it will be withdrawn any time their performance is not up to the standards others set for them.

Emotionally, psychological victims ride a roller-coaster, a wild ride at best. They live the majority of their lives in their own fantasy worlds. They mentally rehearse conversations with people as they expect them to take place. They also live a very push-pull existence which heightens this roller-coaster experience. At one minute they are in prayer and begging God for an opportunity to do something. When that opportunity comes, they try to get out of the very thing they asked for. It seems that the victims' fears and negative self-worth take control, and they believe that God has the same personality as their abusers. Therefore, He is permitting the opportunity only for the purpose of exposing them to open scorn and ridicule.

Here again, if the real causes are not understood, these victims will frustrate their counselors. We could well assume their egos to be so huge and all-consuming that they only wanted to be praised and begged to perform. This is again a lack of understanding, causing the victims more failed relationships. They are then set more deeply into the victim personality mold, and have unintentionally set another person in place as a potential abuser. All because the person in leadership, not understanding, believed that these people needed to have their pride broken and be freed from ignorance!

Victims of psychological abuse often resort to behavior that seems to be provocative and unrealistic, arising out of frustration and continuing feelings of hopelessness. Such unconscious behavior may seem illogical to an objective observer, but often serves to give abusers the excuse needed to attack. The victims are usually sucessful in setting themselves up to receive more abuse and experience more failures.

An unconscious conditioning cycle exists between the abusers and their victims. It works this way:

1. Abusers need someone to blame for their actions, so they goad their victims into misbehaving, so that punishment can occur.

2. Victims need a rationale for the behavior, to excuse the abuse and make it seem to be a proper action.

3. Abusers need to believe that the abuse is justified, that they were doing their victims a favor, making them better people.

4. Victims need the security of knowing what behavior will break the tension and cause the abuse to occur.

5. Victims need to release the guilt they have built up for being bad people.

Victims of psychological abuse, like victims of other types of abuse, seem to need the affirmation of their original abusers. They are not at peace with themselves until they have achieved some measure of approval from that source of abuse. They are willing to go to great lengths for that validation, but in most cases it is never forthcoming. For example, they are driven to consult these abusers before making important decisions. They seem to be saying, "See how much I value you, isn't that worth anything to you?" It can also be an attempt at an insurance policy of sorts, because of the desire to communicate such messages as:

1. "If I follow your advice, I, too, am valuable."
2. "I, too, am someone you can be proud of!"
3. "I am safe now, I am doing everything you think right."

Most of the time, however, this approach has the opposite effect. Abusers assume more and more control, simultaneously robbing the victims of more dignity and self-worth. If the abusers are not the mates, but other family members, the mates lose their influence in the home. They must accept the inferior positions, terminate their relationships with the victims or battle to regain their influence. The mates usually lose, but never before pulling the victims in two, setting them up to receive a whole new load of guilt. Since most victims are already convinced that they are responsible for everything and everyone, this new problem only convicts them further of their failure. It shouts to the victims that they are incapable of sustaining healthy relationships. They become even more convinced that everyone will always dump ON them, or dump THEM.

When the initial abusers are no longer in the picture, the problems do not end—the victims merely look for surrogate abusers. They form these relationships to validate their accomplishments, but the authority figures they choose will also be abusive. And so the cycle begins again. Their problems are now complicated by facts that become true of all victims, regardless of the initial type of abuse. The victims by now have developed psychological needs for abuse. They know just how to provoke abuse, even from non-abusers. When forming relationships, victims are now drawn to those who are abusers.

Sadly, though, even when victims receive approval from surrogates, their views of themselves are never permanently altered. They view themselves as valuable only when someone else says they are, never because inside they think they are. Only the power of God can change their self-images.

Some victims of this abuse will set a certain goal and tell themselves, "If I ever accomplish 'this,' I will have value and worth." But the needs for abuse and punishment have become so powerful that if there are no other abusers available, they will become their own abusers. They will never allow the goal to be successfully fulfilled, but the reasons will seem quite logical. Some of the most common ways in which victims undermine their own goals are:

1. Finding a way to, at the last minute, turn a sure success into unexpected failure.

2. During the process of successfully completing the goal, setting the standards even higher, thus insuring frustration.

3. Deliberately taking on too much responsibility, or spreading themselves too thin and getting into areas beyond their abilities.

What is so difficult to understand is the amount of internal pain victims are willing to suffer, both consciously and subconsciously. However, there are times when victims rise up and set limits to what they will endure, usually when they have reached the proverbial end of their rope. At this point they may find someone who has more authority, or more strength, or someone whom their abusers fear or respect. This person is allowed to intercede and break the abuse cycle. Strangely, this does not violate their needs for abuse, since they still have someone as an authority over them, to control their lives. The product of this momentary release is that even more guilt develops. They believe that they have betrayed their abusers, so they expend extra time and effort making it up to them. Therefore, even release can be a form of abuse. Actually, this break in tension from the outside usually ends up strengthening the control of their abusers, and further intensifies the contempt with which the victims view themselves.

Genesis 16:4-6 records one of the earliest instances of psychological abuse in the Bible: the rivalry between Sarai and Hagar. The situation rapidly escalated in intensity when Sarai, who did not have a victim personality, immediately sought permission to react, and, upon receiving it, once again took control. Note in verse 4 that, when Hagar discovered she was pregnant, she despised Sarai. This word "despised" was used only one other time, when it was repeated by Sarai as she asked Abram for the right of defense. Its meaning is "to abate, bring into contempt, curse or afflict." Apparently Hagar began to attack Sarai, and make her life miserable. Unfortunately, Sarai responded in kind in order to regain control of her servant.

But the problem did not end there. Hagar's bitterness seems to have shaped the nature of her son. In Genesis 21:9 we find Ishmael mocking little Isaac on the day that Isaac was weaned. The full meaning of the word "mocked" as it is used here is derision, making sport of. Galatians 4:28-29 refers to this incident as persecution. The progression seems to be that as the sin of doubt and unbelief entered the life of Sarai she left herself open to be abused. Is it not interesting that, like rebellion, abuse entered this world as a result of sin? Once here, this cycle of abuse never left, but was passed on to Hagar's son, and has affected man from generation to generation ever since.

Once the pattern of abuse entered man's world, it began to appear more frequently, and in its various forms. In a series of incidents recorded about the life of Rebecca, we find Esau using a unique weapon in psychological warfare. First, Genesis 26:34-35 records the fact that the wives Esau chose caused Isaac and Rebecca *"grief of mind."* This phrase means persecution, trouble and bitterness. It is suggested in the Targums that this included quarreling with, and rebelling against, the spiritual beliefs of Isaac and Rebecca. Should it be such a shock that Satan would now expand the areas of abuse? Did not this type of abuse actually begin much earlier, when Esau despised his birthright?

Genesis 27:46 records the depth of depression that the abuse by Esau and his wives brought to Rebecca's personality. She confessed that treatment at their hands made her want to die, just to escape the effect of their influence.

In Genesis 28:8-9 Esau managed to bring the abuse to a new level of intensity. He brought the daughter of his father's first abuser home for the family to cope with for the rest of their lives.

As these events unfolded, the patterns of psychological abuse and its effects are easily traced. First, a young man attacked the very values that set his family apart for God. We found him selling his birthright for food. His concept of its value, as recorded, was that he despised it. How much worry and pain that must have caused! Then he brought women into the family tent who openly made fun of and rebelled against his parents, until Isaac and Rebecca began to show the effects of abuse:

1. Bitterness (how often victims express bitterness and hatred toward their abusers!).
2. Troubled hearts (today we call it anxiety or stress, both powerfully destructive by-products of abuse).
3. Persecution (today we call those who endure such abuse martyrs).
4. Depression.
5. Hopelessness.
6. Suicide.
7. Constantly remembering the failures of the past.
8. Constant opening of past hurts and wounds.

Now consider the relationship between Hannah and Peninnah found in I Samuel 1:2-18. In verse 8 Peninnah is described as Hannah's rival. She provoked Hannah to tears over the issue of Hannah's handicap of not being able to bear children. The results of the psychological abuse in this situation are exposed as follows:

1. Intense, long-term weeping.
2. Loss of appetite.
3. Sorrow of heart.
4. Deep depression.
5. Inferiority.
6. Inability to feel worthy even though she was the favored wife (approval was NOT being expressed by the abuser).
7. Bitterness of soul.
8. Desperation (she went to God to plea for change).
9. Being misunderstood and humiliated in public.
10. Being willing to take radical measures to end the cause of abuse.

As your ministry to abused persons progresses, one of your more startling discoveries may be that symptoms from other personality types are also present in abused victims. In other words, dealing with victim personalities is extremely complicated. You may find dealing with victims of psychological abuse even more complex. These victims have no traumatizing events to point to as a source of their problems. They try to compensate for their internal struggles by involving themselves with very complex reactions, thereby confusing the true source of their problem. That is, they (unconsciously, of course) display one response after the next, attempting to protect themselves. Like other victims, they are afraid that if the truth were exposed everyone would agree with the opinions of their abusers. They believe that everyone would agree that their treatment was within the normal range, that they themselves were weak and irrational in their reactions.

Sometimes it is difficult to avoid being more frustrated by these victims than the others. We often believe that if only they were stronger, they could compensate for this type of abuse. After all, no physical damage occurred. There has been a trend in the body of Christ in recent years to overlook the emotional part of man. All we succeed in doing is to ignore a powerful one-third of each person created in the image and likeness of Almighty God. We send people forward into a love relationship with the living God, and then tell them to ignore that love, not to feel or respond to it! Is the level of both frustration and death in the body today any wonder? What damage this viewpoint does not do is easily finished off by the fact that we offer little or no ministry to damaged emotions. How do we expect the church to be excited about our God? On the one hand we say, "Careful, do not get carried away, feelings are totally undependable." And on the other hand, we say, "Worship and love the Lord as a bride does a groom." All the while we offer no healing for the feelings, the fears, the unhealthy emotions that keep so many in such complex pain and turmoil. Often they are afraid even to ask for help, because the church has declared emotion to be carnal and unspiritual and even disgraceful.

Listed below are some characteristics of psychologically abused victims. Be on the lookout for these:

1. Fear of forming a close relationship with God because He is untrustworthy.
2. Feeling able to receive only punishment from God.
3. Lack of understanding of God's standards of behavior, and so believing that they always fail.
4. Inability to receive love from God or to love themselves.
5. Having difficulty expressing emotion.
6. Fear of criticism or evaluation of any type.
7. Fear of authority and anyone in authority.
8. An honest conviction that they can do nothing that will measure up to any standards.
9. Oversensitivity to a weakness or handicap.

10. Intense need for reinforcement, but no sign that confidence is building.

11. Always assuming blame for any problem or situation, particularly those involving authority figures.

12. Believing only bad about themselves.

13. Having the opinion of only one person as their only true standard.

14. Striving always to be perfect.

15. Striving to please one particular person, even through irrational behavior.

16. Deep sorrow that has no identifiable cause.

17. Constant battle with low self-estem and self-worth.

18. Constant struggle against negative thoughts.

19. Willingness to receive strong and undeserved criticism from one person.

20. Body stance that says, "I am sorry I exist."

21. Many of the physical traits of the physically abused.

When ministering to these victims, break the spirit and power of their abusers over them. Also break the power of their words spoken over the victims. Other spirits you may find are:

1. Fear of people.
2. Fear of failure, and failure.
3. Fear of authority.
4. Fear of success.
5. Fear of exposure.
6. Self-hatred.
7. Inferiority.
8. Worthlessness.
9. Unloved and unwanted.
10. Rejection, and fear of rejection.
11. Hurt and wounded.
12. Depression.
13. Hopeless and helpless.
14. Suicide.

15. Sorrow and mourning.
16. Negative (that is correct).
17. Pain or the need for pain.

As the ministry progresses, spirits that are specific to the degree of psychological abuse suffered will become obvious and will need to be dealt with. Pay particular attention to the different fears present, which will depend on the methods of control the abusers used. The list will also vary if their abusers used either physical or sexual abuse. As with the other victims, these were probably abused as children. Break the spirit and power of the orginal abusers over them, then minister to any areas that relate to the initial abuse.

Please read carefully the section on aftercare. These "victims" will need tender loving care and much patience as their complete healing becomes manifest.

Chapter 12

SPOUSE ABUSE

Spouse abuse is one of the fastest-growing problems affecting American families today. Therefore, this section on the victim personality would not be complete without a consideration of this extremely disturbing behavior. These family situations are becoming more complex, and gaining more national media attention as professionals who regularly deal with people in crisis are realizing the extent of the damage. Some people seem to have a compelling need for a continuing abusive relationship in their environment. As this problem is being more widely observed and dealt with, we now realize that the type of cyclic abuse we refer to as spouse abuse is no longer limited to marriage! Abuse is occurring in dating relationships, relationships among roommates, in friendships and even in the workplace. We are coming to understand that a victim will even abuse himself if there is no other abuser available. This chapter is not intended to provide a complete study of this problem, nor will every symptom be described, nor every variation of the abuse cycle be delineated. We will only attempt to discuss the variety of causes, and the symptoms will be listed in their order of severity.

It is important to be aware that the abuser has as many problems, and as much need for ministry, as does the victim. They are usually found married to each other, dating or living with each other because of these long-term problems. (The only exception seems to be the person whose spiritual heritage included a victim personality, but who was somehow immune to that portion of his inheritance.)

Even though the problem is not a new one (at least two

cases are recorded in the Bible) it has now caught the concern of leading treatment professionals around the country. Not many days go by without the news recording a murder or attempted murder due to spouse abuse. Have you noticed the number of news programs and documentaries being produced concerning the battered wife and battered husband syndrome? This is now considered a viable defense for some family murders! Consider then: How long will it be before this becomes a valid defense in murder or attempted murder cases involving dating partners, roommates or employer-employee relationships?

Large segments of society are now recognizing, and rightfully so, the severe damage that both psychological and physical abuse cause, damage not only to the body but also to the mind, will and emotions. Is it any wonder, then, that the victim's behavior is seriously altered as he reaches his level of tolerance? We submit that the soul of a person who has experienced abuse in any form is so scarred that only the power of God can bring healing. Even so, in order to realize complete restoration, there will be a need for much continuing care and support by the persons ministering to the victim, and by his Christian family.

How often do you read magazine and newspaper articles addressing this problem, offering one solution after another but with little or no real success from any solution? As leaders and pastors, how often are you now being faced with such problems? If we are honest, most of us feel totally inadequate in dealing with the enormity or the complexity of these situations. And we are even more troubled, confused and perplexed by the exposure of abuse in the lives of ministers and leaders and their families. However, there is great hope and effective freedom available the moment we admit our inadequacies, no matter that we are supposed to have all the answers already! PRAISE GOD!

There seem to be certain questions asked regularly of

those who have lived in an abusive situation. Let us now list, then deal with, some of these so that you can begin to understand why abuse is becoming so widespread.

1. Why do these victims remain in abusive situations, particularly with divorce so rampant today?

2. Was the partner abusive prior to marriage or prior to a commitment being made?

3. What originally attracted the victim to the abuser?

4. How do the victims view themselves? What is their own level of self-worth?

5. Why do the victims not report their problem to a social agency, or to the police?

6. What makes most victims keep their situations a secret, even from family and close friends?

7. For what reasons do most victims deny the abuse, even when questioned by someone trained to recognize the symptoms?

8. Is there any damage to children living in such an environment? If there is, why is help not sought for the sake of the children?

9. What are the greatest fears of the victim?

10. Why do many victims create such extensive webs of protection for the abuser?

11. What produces such intense feelings of guilt and responsibility within the victim for the abuser's actions?

12. What causes one human being to believe that he has any right to abuse another human being?

13. How do the abusers feel about themselves and about their victims?

14. Are either the victim OR the abuser in control of the situation?

15. Are both the victim and the abuser in the situation because they enjoy it, or derive from it some satisfaction?

16. What happens if one gets help and the other does not?

17. What changes have occurred within the family

unit to cause this problem, or even to allow its existence?

18. What can be done for both the victim and the abuser?

QUESTION 1.

Why do these victims remain in abusive situations, particularly with divorce so rampant today?

The connections between past emotional trauma, past life experience and present life choices must be explored. Most victims living in abusive situations (whether those situations involve mental, physical or sexual abuse) all have at least one common base root. The most universal roots are:

A. They were abused in some manner growing up, and received little or no help prior to forming the present abusive relationship.

B. They grew up observing regular bouts of some form of abuse in their families.

C. One or both of their parents were addictive or compulsive, with all the effects of that type of personality.

D. They were shattered by a traumatic event or events, resulting in their own self-worth being undermined or destroyed.

E. Their spiritual inheritance included a victim personality, so they find themselves constantly involved with abusers, for no discernible reason. (Please refer to the exception noted at the beginning of this chapter. For a complete explanation concerning inherited iniquity, please refer to the chapter dealing with iniquity.)

As has been explained in the three preceding chapters on physical, sexual and psychological abuse, a victim's personality becomes warped as a result of the abuse. Restoration requires God's power in bringing freedom and healing to the core of the individual's mind, will, emotions and spirit. If that freedom is not received, the victim grows up unconsciously convinced (being strongly influenced by demonic spirits) that he deserves regular abuse because he is inherently evil or inferior. He is convinced that without that abuse he could not be trusted to behave in a manner acceptable to society. Often the abuse, or threat of abuse, acts as structure for its victims. As difficult as it is to understand, the victim usually feels that life continues in a comfortably secure pattern only when an abuser is in the picture somewhere. So it is that, without conscious awareness, victims will always draw at least one abuser of some type into their lives. All the areas in which the victim needs God's freedom work like magnets to attract those with a need to abuse.

Another interesting fact is that most victims will themselves become abusers, given the right circumstances. That is one reason why most statistics published prove that over 95% of abused children become abusive parents.

Therefore, when victims say they cannot explain why, but they CANNOT leave their abusers, or they return time and time again to the abusers, in spite of logic and support from you, they are being more truthful than either of you realize. We must understand the strength of the attack on their minds, wills and emotions by these evil spirits, as well as the pull and drawing power. Often it is impossible for these victims even to make intelligent decisions, much less stick with them. We feel strongly that the existence of these spirits is the reason that some victims cannot even make an attempt to separate from their abusers, or in other cases will divorce the abuser only to marry another one. We dealt with one victim who was married to her fifth abuser! This also explains why shelters for battered women see such high rates of return visits by the same victims. This high return rate is one of the major factors in frustration and even burnout for those working with victims.

QUESTION 2

Was the partner abusive prior to marriage or prior to a commitment being made?

Usually the victim had some indication of the abuser's nature, but, in all fairness to the victim, several factors must be considered. You must have some degree of understanding and compassion for how and why they got themselves into this mess when the symptoms are obvious, even to casual observers! This should also help you understand why some people make choices against your advice.

A. Often the victims do not realize that abusive treatment is not normal. It was the pattern in their families and is what they received growing up.

B. They have experienced trauma and abuse to such an extent that they now accept and expect it. They believe something to be wrong within themselves.

C. Their formative years were so full of psychological abuse, and it so damaged their own self-images, that they accept abusive relationships as the best available to them.

D. They believed that they could change the behavior of the abuser.

E. Those spirits served as such a powerful drawing force that, no matter what the victims perceived, they could not resist being attracted to the abusers.

F. The victims themselves believe that if things are going well for them, then something terrible is about to happen. Therefore THEY set up the something terrible: the ever-present abusers. This gives them some sense of control in their lives even though the thought processes are completely unconscious.

G. The ability of the victims to objectively evaluate the abusers' behavior is seriously impaired. It is a sad but true illustration of the very blindness of love.

At this point allow us to introduce several possibilities that would frustrate you in working with either the victims of abuse or the abusers themselves. Many pastors and counselors have been so hurt and so burned by so many of these victims that they have quit the battle completely! This problem affects many in the body of Christ, including leaders; surely it is one of Satan's favorite ploys! We suggest that he is well aware that if he can keep such numbers of people bound up, frustrated and causing difficulties among God's people, then we ourselves will actually limit the power of the church in the world today.

Therefore, we who have the opportunity to minister not only God's freedom but His healing to both the victim and the abuser must understand them. They often feel totally out of control of their lives, their choices and also their behavior. They are as frustrated themselves as they are frustrating to you. Their levels of frustration and fear are so high that they often push away those trying to help, or they attempt to make their counselors into villains, responsible for all the problems and poor choices of the victims . . . even responsible for the behavior of the abusers.

Another obstacle in working with victims or abusers is that they tend to demand all your time and attention. If it is not forthcoming, they want you to feel guilty for the time you are not with them. Should such a situation occur, realize that victims are not terrible people, nor are you a manipulative or controlling counselor. The spirits influencing them bring such fear and confusion that the poor victims dare not trust their own ability to make correct decisions. They may even seem to be operating from feelings of jealousy or malicious intent toward you and your efforts to help. Actually, they are in great need of emotional support and feel that everything in their lives that has been a positive statement of their value or worth has been removed. Most people with these problems believe that, since something is inherently wrong with them, anyone who really gets to know them will either begin to dislike them, disapprove of them, be ashamed of them, distrust them or tire of being with them and go in search of someone more acceptable. Therefore they will view any change in the amount of time you spend with them as a reflection on them.

QUESTION 3

What originally attracted the victim to the abuser?

Most of the time the reason for their attraction to each other is totally unconscious. When pushed they respond with "I do not know" or with a seemingly logical response. However, the truth lies first in the spiritual realm, then secondly in the realm of a scarred and damaged personality. In the realm of the spirit, we find "deep calling to deep"—meaning that the spirits that have influenced the mind, will, and emotions of the victims attract the spirits that influence the mind, will, and emotions of the abusers. It seems to the two involved that fate or circumstances put them together and that they could not help themselves.

Also, the victims usually have such low self-images that they feel more comfortable with someone who agrees with their own opinions of themselves. They also need someone to balance areas of success or approval. The only way victims can allow even one area of success is to be receiving abuse in another. If that abuse is not supplied by an outside party, they begin to set failure in motion themselves.

The abusers, on the other hand, because of their own problems of insecurity and low self-esteem, require someone in their environment whom they can "lord it over" and abuse in one way or another. Thereby they gain some sense of worth.

QUESTION 4

How do the victims view themselves? What is their own level of self-worth?

Most victims view themselves as failures. They truly believe that once you get to know them better you will dislike them, find them boring, realize that their capabilities are much less than what you thought, discover that they are evil and to be avoided or punished, agree that great calamity naturally follows them. They are quite sure that you will conclude that they deserve nothing good, but that should good befall them, something terrible will soon happen to even out the score. They expect you to learn that they bring out the worst in their abusers, that if the abusers were with someone else they would be perfectly normal.

QUESTION 5

Why do victims not report their problem to a social agency, or to the police?

To answer this question we must explain how the thought processes of victims have become so confused and distorted that simple conclusions are beyond their reach!

A. Since most victims erroneously assume that their abusers would behave normally with anyone else, they believe that anyone to whom they reported the abuse would automatically blame them for the problem. It often happens!

This "reasoning" comes as a result of the following:

1. The abusers continually tell the victims that their actions provoked the abuse, and that it was punishment they brought on themselves!

2. The abusers continually point out that the weaknesses of the victims place intolerable stresses on the abusers.

3. The abusers continually remind their victims that they themselves are deeply loved and respected by others.

4. Since most adult victims spent many of their younger years as victims, their resulting lack of self-worth causes them to accept blame for the abuse.

The fact that law-enforcement agencies, courts, and

social service departments were for so many years reluctant to become involved in domestic problems has further reinforced the victims' convictions that they would not be believed anyway. Fortunately the situation is changing as more attention is at last being focused on the abuse issue.

Most victims saw the church as totally unprepared to deal with abusive situations, and most leaders as intimidated by the entire issue. For years the church has blinded its eyes to abuse in its midst. Should such a case have become unavoidable, it would have been treated as such an exception that both the victim and abuser would have ended up more frustrated and wounded than ever.

B. Such a cycle of fear has been formed by the abusers that victims are convinced that the abuse would be many times worse should it be reported.

If abusers ever suspect that their victims even hinted to anyone (family, friend, minister or neighbor) the truth about them, the abuse becomes much more brutal and intense. Actually, most victims never drop such hints in the first place. But after a while victims begin to reason along this line: If the abuse has become THIS bad and I was innocent, think how awful it would be if I did tell someone!

C. If there are children in the family, abusers usually convince their victims that if they report the abuse or dare to leave:
   1. Authorities would take the children.
   2. The abusers would get custody.
   3. The abusers would disappear with the children.

Bearing in mind that most victims already feel inferior and unacceptable to society, one can see what a simple matter it is for abusers to convince them that they would lose everything. It has also been the approach of abusers to exact loyalty from the children, based on:

   1. Fear of the abusers.

2. Constant reinforcement of the childrens' inferiority.

3. The children's need for the abuser's approval for their own validation.

D. The abusers usually convince their victims that all the family, even extended family members, love the abusers more and would defend the abusers to the authorities!

This opinion can be successfully formed by isolating the victims, then persuading *them* to take responsibility for the withdrawal. Also, it can be accomplished because most people exposed to such abuse have lived like this for years and assume it to be normal. Some counselors are themselves intimidated by the abusers, or, worse yet, fear that if they interfere they will lose contact with the victims altogether. Perhaps they do not understand why the victims tolerate such mistreatment in the first place, and conclude that they must want it to continue. All these reactions do is to reinforce the victims' belief that no one will rise to their defense.

E. The abusers convince the victims that it will be the victims locked up, not the abusers!

F. If the abuse is sexual or psychological the victims are convinced by the abusers that the abuse could never be proved.

This is heightened in the cases of sexual abuse if the parties involved are of consenting age, married, or in an ongoing dating arrangement. The abusers convince their victims that what goes on between committed adults is governed by no laws or statutes. This is *not* true! There are many cases now being tried and WON of both date and marriage rape!

G. If the abuse occurs on the job or in a friendship the abusers convince their victims that no one will take the situation seriously and that the victims will be viewed as weak fools.

This is still very true in our society. Victims are not

viewed as people who need ministry. We tend to judge them harshly and expect them to extricate themselves from any problem relationships. After all, this is America and they are free! Their staying is misinterpreted as wanting abuse.

QUESTION 6

What makes most victims keep their situations a secret, even from family and close friends?

Most victims are afraid that if the persons they tell do believe them, those persons will immediately demand that the victims do something about their own situations. This is impossible in the minds of most victims, for one or all the following reasons:

A. They feel totally dependent on the abusers and do not believe that they could make it without them.

B. If this is a marriage or dating relationship they honestly believe themselves to be deeply in love.

C. They believe that the one in whom they confide their abuse will openly confront the abusers, causing all contacts between themselves and the confidante to be terminated by the abusers.

D. Some are reluctant to expose the abusers because they do not want that person to be disliked and disapproved.

E. The victims suffer such shame and guilt that they are afraid they will lose the love, support, and respect of anyone they might tell. In their minds, this is too high a price to pay.

F. Victims are afraid that, should word of their verbal "betrayal" get back to their abusers, reprisal would follow and the abuse would intensify.

G. If this is a work, dating, friendship, or roommate situation, victims are afraid that even if they are believed there will be little or no help for them, because everyone will just suggest counseling. Therefore, it seems to them that the abusers get away without paying any price at all, or having any stigma attached to them, while the victims take the whole load!

QUESTION 7

For what reasons do most victims deny the abuse, even when questioned by someone trained to recognize the symptoms?

Victims are very much afraid of the unknown, of life without their abusers, especially in marriage. They also worry about what will be legally required of them, and that worry is heightened in employee-employer situations. Also, they are terrified of reprisal.

QUESTION 8

Is there any damage to children living in such an environment? If there is, why is help not sought for the sake of the children?

YES, there is damage to the children, usually extensive, and not easily dealt with! Herein lies the reason we see abusive situations repeat themselves for generation after generation. The more tense and volatile the American family becomes, the more violently the members feel free to treat one another. It almost seems that we have on our hands a generation of adults who feel complete freedom to act out their frustrations and aggressions on each other! The more violence that children in these situations observe, the more will this behavior repeat itself as they become adults.

It is true that without the power of God we do to others *exactly* what was done to us. We do not know any better. Bearing this truth in mind, it then becomes easy to understand why most adult victims were childhood victims, and almost *all* adult abusers were childhood victims as well. In addition, now understanding that the need to be someone's victim can be handed down as family inheritance, is it any wonder that abuse in all forms is rapidly spreading in our country?

Most victims as well as most abusers do not believe that

real help is available. They accept the problems as within their own personalities. They bought Satan's lies that he has put out through both the media and secular counselors that "there are some things for which there are no real and lasting cures." They become paralyzed by their own sense of hopelessness. They also are terrified that if anyone knew what went on behind closed doors they would end up losing the very children they want to help.

QUESTION 9

What are the greatest fears of the victims?

These fears can most often be delineated among victims:

A. Fear that they will never be believed or taken seriously by any helping agency.

B. Fear that the abuse will be much worse if they do report it.

C. Fear that their abusers are right and it will be discovered that everything really is the fault of the victims.

D. Fear that they cannot survive emotionally without the abusers.

E. Fear that they cannot make it alone financially.

F. Fear that they have lost all control over their own lives, and would no longer be able to exercise that control should it be restored to them.

G. Fear that they can no longer think clearly due to the continuous anxiety they suffer.

H. Fear of the unknown.

I. Fear that they are the sole parties responsible for the existing situation. Belief that they have to keep everything together for the sake of everyone involved. The guilt of ruining all these lives is more than they can face.

J. Fear that they can do nothing to alter the situation anyway, so they take on a very passive personality.

K. Fear that the abuser will change and they will miss out on a perfect situation just because they could not wait long enough!

L. Fear that because they probably have been victims all their lives, God intended them always to be victims, and that nothing will ever change except the identity of the abuser.

As you can discern, God must heal many areas of the victims' personalities as well as deliver them from their spiritual and physical needs for tormentors. They will need as much of your love, care, and time as will the abusers themselves!

QUESTION 10

Why do many victims create such extensive webs of protection for the abuser?

Anxiety can reach such a peak in personalities of victims that they are less fearful of living with their abusers than without! They feel a need to protect the abuser at all costs so that the relationship remains intact! (The only exception to this is when they fear or respect another authority figure more than the abusers. They then will allow that other source of strength to influence a change in their situation.) When the victims know the whereabouts of the abusers and can plot the abusers' courses of action by observing their behavior daily, only then is their stress lessened. Most people working with victims accept this type of reasoning as a cover-up for their desire to remain in abusive situations. They do not understand the level of terror nor the predictability of the cycle of abusive behavior. However, please realize that this is an effect of abuse on the soul and spirit of its victims, not their desire to remain involved with abusers. Later we will delineate the cyclic pattern of abuse.

After a period of repeated abuse a victim usually adopts a very passive personality and the abuser becomes the one who takes action, makes most of the decisions, and chooses the direction and goals. The victims become almost paralyzed in their roles of response rather than initiative. This causes the victims to believe that without the abusers they would be incapable of successfully carrying out their everyday lives. At this point most victims accept themselves as failures and cease attempting to function without their abusers.

The situation has now deteriorated to such a one-sided level of nonfuctioning that the victims have taken on mental attitudes of learned helplessness. They are so terrified to be without the abusers that to admit to the problem seems more dangerous than does the actual abuse.

QUESTION 11

What produces such intense feelings of guilt and responsibility within the victims for the abusers' actions?

The victims of continuous abuse have developed such low self-esteem that they have no idea that most of what they experience is not brought on by themselves. Their usual reasoning is that if they were a better person or a stronger-willed person, then these things would not happen to them. Their abusers have usually pointed out every flaw conceivable to reinforce the victims' ineffectiveness. If there are no mistakes or weaknesses to point out, often the abusers will resort to treating their victims like children and blaming them for all the stress. This implies that the abuse was the result of the victims' poor behavior traits. After a period of time of constantly being blamed for the abusers' moods and actions, as well as having every flaw real or imagined blown up out of proportion, victims take on total blame for their abuse. It must again be emphasized that most adult victims were first child victims. Be aware, then, that you are dealing with a well-reinforced concept of worthlessness within these victims. Furthermore, most of them have been abused for so many years that they quite naturally accept all the blame and all the guilt!

Often it is difficult for an observer to understand. What has happened as a result of such trauma is that the victims' abilities to reason clearly have been clouded by oppressive evil spirits. These literally distort their perception of reality to the point that the abusers' views of them become their own! This is further complicated by the necessity for some of the spirits within the victims to control the actions of the abusers.

QUESTION 12

What causes one human being to believe that he has any right to abuse another human being?

The abusive personality will be fully considered in another chapter. Remember for now that a large percentage of abusers were themselves victims. This is not stated to justify or excuse their behavior, but to lay a foundation of understanding and concern. As leaders we will be in situations to minister the freedom of Jesus Christ to the victims and also to the abusers. We cannot unless we realize that in most cases the roots are the same!

Let us take a quick look at the most common causes for abuse, leaving the details for the next chapter:

A. Abusers are only expressing what they have experienced or observed as proper behavior.

B. Most do not want to behave as they do, but driving forces inside of them take control and they feel totally out of control themselves.

C. Many are haunted by as many feelings of inferiority and failure as their victims. The only way they know to feel like they have any worth is to make someone else feel more worthless than they do.

D. They require someone to blame for the feelings of failure that shout at them constantly.

E. Some need to inflict pain on someone else to alleviate some of their own.

F. Many are reacting to the drawing need of the spirits that oppress their victims.

QUESTION 13

How do the abusers feel about themselves and about their victims?

In many cases the abusers feel as disgusted by their behavior as we do as observers and are crying out for help, love, understanding, and acceptance. These feelings are intense during what we call the honeymoon stage. At other stages they feel totally justified for their actions and do not understand anyone being upset over their behavior. In fact, during these later stages they are convinced that if you knew the victims as they do you would understand completely and might even abuse them yourself! Then there are stages where their own level of frustration is so high that they are unable to deal adequately with their anger and rage. It is at these times that they will take on all comers.

At other times they are so grateful to the victims for staying with them that they cannot love them enough or do enough for them. During this stage the victims are treated so well that it actually serves as an anchor to keep them in the relationship. Some victims finally reach a point of pushing the cycle of abuse to the actual abuse stage, to "get it over with," knowing that this is the next part of the cycle.

Most abusers also have a very loving, warm, and caring side to their natures. However, the more they progress into the abusive side of their personalities the less that kindness appears.

Their views of the victims change based on where they are in the abuse cycle. Sometimes they are so grateful and loving toward the victims because of their display of loyalty. At other times they believe that their victims should be glad the abusers stick with them since the victims are so difficult to live with! At still other times they hate the victims and believe that if the victims were not with them they would not be engaging in such awful behavior. Or they believe that the victims are terrible drains, and they wish they *would* separate. There may even be a point where the abusers have such little respect for their victims that they are brutal, humiliating, and psychologically violent in their descriptions of the victims and their worth.

QUESTION 14

Are either the victim OR the abuser in control of the situation?

It looks like the two alternate control, but in reality the oppressive spirits that torment BOTH of them are actually in control.

QUESTION 15

Are both the victim and the abuser in the situation because they enjoy it, or derive from it some satisfaction?

Neither one likes nor enjoys it at all. The evil, oppressive spirits harassing both parties need for the situations to continue. They know how to drive both parties into action.

QUESTION 16

What happens if one gets help and the other does not?

If the relationships continue, those who received ministry will experience such attitude and self-image changes that they will neither react nor respond to the same stimuli in the same old manner.

When the VICTIMS receive effective ministry, the following are among the first changes to be noticed:

A. The need to be constant failures gradually ceases. Less often do they set themselves up to fail either consciously or unconsciously.

B. Their self-images gradually improve so that the victims no longer believe they deserve the abuse.

C. Their thought processes clear and no longer do they see themselves as helpless and without alternatives.

D. They attain a new level of reality, and in the process realize that they WILL be believed.

E. The level of guilt they have lived under disappears and they no longer feel responsible for the behavior of the abusers.

F. At this point of development they begin to force the abusers to also seek and receive freedom. They become so convinced that change is possible that they either lead the abusers to receive help or the abusers are forced to find other victims.

Caution: there is a crucial point in the healing process when victims begin to feel guilty, and wonder if they should compromise their healthier outlooks to again include their abusers. Particularly is this likely if a separation is occurring; they begin to believe that they are ruining the lives of others. This is definitely possible if children are involved, or a closeness exists with extended family. If this separation entails divorce, all parties who have a deep relationship with Jesus will take on tremendous spiritual guilt, and place themselves in danger of returning to situations that would undo their healing and deliverance.

When those receiving help are the ABUSERS, the following are among the first changes to be noticed:

A. They no longer are driven by such intense feelings of inferiority.

B. The internal rage and hurt begin to subside and the need to express their own frustations in violence decreases.

C. They no longer panic at admitting mistakes or failures; therefore their need for scapegoats no longer exists.

D. Healing occurs in their minds and emotions, bringing freedom. They no longer need to try so hard to act as they think adults would.

E. The more healing they receive, the more respect they develop for themselves, thereby producing a respect for the lives, minds and bodies of their victims. This acts as a brake to halt abusive behavior.

F. As the need to abuse decreases, the victims (if they have not received ministry) begin to feel very unsure of themselves and begin to provoke the abusers into abusive action. If this begins to occur it is primarily because the victims no longer know what to expect, and the unknown is too full of fear for them. Some of them have so identified with abuse that they no longer feel loved or wanted if it stops!

G. The former abusers, like the freed victims, become so excited by their new feelings and responses that they begin to force their victims to get help!

QUESTION 17

What changes have occurred within the family unit to cause this problem, or to allow its existence?

As has been stated in the chapters dealing with iniquity, as each generation engages in the sins and behaviors of the preceding generations, the problems multiply. More people are involved in the problems and are bound by the effects of the problems, so Satan has more opportunity to attack and destroy what God created to be good and pleasant. Furthermore, as each generation compromises further the laws of God, more sin, more violence, more breakdown of the family and relationships occur. It seems that the more respect and love we lose for our Creator, the more hatred we feel free to express toward His creation and its rules and standards. The more this occurs, the more stress the family and interpersonal relationships must endure. It is as though we are so frustrated, so confused and hurt inside that the only way some of us can exist is to act out our violence. Somehow we think that this will alleviate some of our internal pressure.

QUESTION 18

What can be done for both the victim and the abuser?

Both groups need to be introduced to the help available in the power of the life of Jesus Christ! Both must be willing to admit that they have a problem requiring deliverance and healing. As leaders placed by God into their lives, you must gently but firmly bring them to a point of realizing that their behavior is a result of their experiences, and that help and change *are* available in Jesus Christ! In addition, you must let them know that it is a process, that it requires work, commitment, time, and a determined willingness to break habits once they have received ministry. They must know that there is no "Magic Wand" to wave over them for instant recovery, but that they must be prepared to accept the responsibilities of wholeness. They must walk through it and walk it out. They must also know that you will be there for them as they gain spiritual strength.

The cycle of abuse referred to earlier will now be described. Please understand that the length of the cycle can be as long as five to ten years from its beginning to its completion, or as short as an hour in cases of severe stress or if the problems have become extremely severe.

I. The stage of verbal or non-verbal threat of abuse begins, involving:
    A. Increased verbal altercations.
    B. Changes forced into the routine schedules.
    C. Minor physical attacks.

II. The abusers begin to be more and more psychologically abusive.
    A. They may begin to threaten to hurt someone close to the victims.
    B. They begin to humiliate the victims in public as well as in private.
    C. Verbal harangues begin.
    D. Seeing the victims beginning to react in anger, they begin to push the victims even more to give themselves an exuse for abuse.
    E. Under tension victims give the abusers the excuses they have been waiting for, and the actual abuse begins.

(This and the next stage are accelerated by victims of long standing who want the battering stages over and done so the honeymoon stage can begin again.)

III. Intense abuse

A. This stage usually begins when the abusers have reached the end of their coping strengths and want to teach the victims a lesson, make a point, or administer punishment for the victims' behavior.

B. Either during or just after the abuse the abusers instruct their victims as to which of the victims' actions made the abuse necessary.

C. As the victims learn what to expect, they may push this stage by doing things to provoke the abuse. They resort to such measures only to get the pain over with.

IV. Honeymoon stage

A. Usually this stage is filled with promises to get help, emotional and often tearful vows that abuse will never happen again.

B. Abusers are extremely kind and contrite; they even may confess their problem to someone and show a great deal of emotion.

C. At times they will involve family members to convince the victims that they are serious and to get the victim to stay with them.

D. They might even contact a spiritual leader, asking him or her to convince the victims to remain.

E. To "prove" their seriousness, they may temporarily give up something or alter their behavior patterns. For example:

1. They may get a job or a better job.

2. They may give up an addictive habit.

3. They may renew their commitment to the victim (even stop dating other people, if appropriate).

4. They may even cease those activities on which they blame the internal stress that (they say) causes the abuse.

Be on the alert for the following symptoms in anyone whom you suspect may be a victim. These usually accompany severe abuse:

A. Sleeplessness, abnormal sleep habits or patterns.

B. Compulsive sleeping, with the excuse of always being tired.

C. Either no appetite or a compulsion to eat everything in sight.

D. Constant physical ailments such as:

   1. Stomach problems.

   2. High blood pressure.

   3. Heart palpitations.

   4. Anxiety attacks.

   5. Stress-related attacks of all types.

Please note that most victims deny (even to themselves) the reality of the intense stage of abuse and its effects.

In I Samuel 25:3-42 we find a record of a wife whose husband was well known for his cruel actions and attitudes. The record begins by stating in verse 3 that Nabal's wife, Abigail, was "of good understanding and a beautiful countenance." In the orginal language, "of good understanding" actually means a good person who is also filled with intelligence and wisdom. Nabal, on the other hand, is described as churlish, which literally means cruel, hard, grievous and rough. He was evil in everything he did. In verses 10-11 we are given a picture of his abuse, even to men who had done him a great service. He lived up to his reputation. That description is reiterated in verses 14-17 by the servant, who stated that Nabal flew at David's men in a rage, and went on with freedom to say that Nabal was an evil and wicked man and completely unreasonable.

It is obvious that everyone, including Abigail, had been a victim of Nabal's abuse. The servant was free to address Abigail as a fellow sufferer, even cautioning her about what to do. In verses 18-25 Abigail went to David in secret in an attempt to make amends for Nabal's behavior. She made excuses for him, she took responsibility for his evil ways, and she appealed to David's good character. In the course of her plea she actually stated that Nabal could not help himself, for he lived up to the expectations of his parents: his name means "foolishly wicked."

Abigail twice expressed fear of her husband. In verse 18 she departed secretly, actually sneaked off, sending the servants ahead so that, if she were caught, the servants might escape and get to David. In verse 37 she came home to find Nabal very drunk, and so she waited until morning to tell him what she had done. Nabal reacted in such anger that his heart hardened within him like stone, and he died ten days later.

Here was a wise and beautiful woman living with a violent and abusive man. She went to great lengths to protect him from himself, even to the point of risking her own safety. She and the rest of the household obviously lived in fear of this man, dominated by his rage and violence, his abusive behavior.

Like most victims she accepted responsibility for his behavior, tried to explain it away and appease the person she knew could bring destruction to the entire household. Here God draws a picture of His plan. He wants to:

A. Deliver the victims from all ramifications of the abusers' behavior.

B. Save their lives from any more physical or emotional pain.

C. Protect them from the reactions of their abusers when it is learned that they have been to the King for help.

D. Deliver them from fear.

E. Redeem their lives by the life of the King.

F. Give them entirely new types of relationships.

G. Establish new lifestyles.

H. Give them an emotional relationship with the King of kings by establishing trust and communion.

In I Kings chapters 16-21 we are introduced to Queen Jezebel, a woman physically and psychologically abusive.

She put fear not only into her own husband but the entire kingdom, including the prophet of God. Her violence was well known and one threat sent the man of God running for his very life. If we take a quick look at the result of living with an abuser over a long period of time, we will find that Ahab had a very low self-image and that by chapter 19 we find a man totally incapable of functioning.

In chapter 18 a showdown took place between the prophets of Baal and God's prophet, Elijah. King Ahab agreed to the terms set out by Elijah, the contest was held, and God triumphed mightily. The prophets of Baal were killed; then God sent rain, after a drought of three years. King Ahab went home happy that the rain came but terrified that he now had to tell Jezebel her prophets were dead. So in verse 1 of chapter 19 we find him telling Jezebel that Elijah killed all the prophets, but he neglected to mention his agreement to the rules of the contest, as well as his promise for the two of them to return to the living God if Elijah did win.

Fear of her abuse so paralyzed him that:
A. He could not keep his commitment to God. (It is not uncommon for victims to see their abusers as a bigger reality and a greater threat than God.)
B. He could not effectively run the country if its running violated her desires. (It is not uncommon to find victims more eager to meet the needs of their abusers than to meet their other responsibilities.)
C. He could not admit his own involvement in the day's events. (It is unusual for victims to admit to their own actions. They have strong parent-child relationships with their abusers and must have their approval at all costs.)

Fear of the abuser had such an effect on Elijah that:
A. He lost all sight of who he was in God. His ability to reason was so clouded that he forgot all that God had just done. (It happens often that abusers cause their victims to be unable to reason clearly.)

B. He ran rather then face her anger.

C. He began to doubt God's care for him. (Often the victims' views of God are so distorted that they believe that God intends them to be abused. Some of them even believe that God's nature is also that of the abusers.)

In chapter 21 we see the severe end of some victims:

A. Ahab had reached the state of being so frustrated with life that if he did not get what he wanted (no matter whether right or wrong) he could not cope.

B. He was so plagued by severe depression that he retreated to his bed.

C. He had regressed to the immaturity level of a small child, as his self-esteem lowered.

D. He was so involved with his abuser that he did not question the level of abuse she inflicted.

E. He did exactly what she told him to do.

F. He was completely under her control, even to accepting her value system.

G. When questioned he saw nothing wrong in her behavior.

When ministering to victims you must discover not only the present causes but also the orginal roots, remembering that adult victims were usually childhood victims. The following is a list of evil spirits that may be present:

A. Fear of the attacker. Break the "spirit and power of" the abusers over their victims, calling them by name if known.

B. Fear of attack.

C. Fear of pain.

D. King of terrors.

E. Fear of failure.

F. Fear of success.

G. Fear of people.

H. Fear of shame and exposure.

I. Unloved and unwanted.

J. Rejection and fear of rejection.

K. Worthlessness and unworthiness.
L. Guilt and a false sense of responsibility.
M. False reality.
N. Lying.
O. Self-hatred.
P. Anger, rage, violence.
Q. Bitterness and resentment.

When ministering to victims, remember that they have such low self-images and self-esteems that they require continual reinforcement for a time. While deliverance is a giant step forward for them, and of vital importance to their recovery, it is actually just the beginning. They will need much healing, much patience and love in the months ahead. The results make your efforts well worth it. Sometimes it is like watching the loveliest red roses blossoming before your very eyes!

Chapter 13

THE ABUSER

Without including a chapter dealing with the abusers themselves, this section would be incomplete, even biased in its presentation of the different forms of abuse. Most leaders, at some time in their lives, have been pressured by abusers in places of influence. Consequently, they have formed opinions of the abusive personality out of their own hurts and frustrations. We can well understand that their ministry to abusers is without large doses of empathy. We pray that, after reading the material in this chapter, a new understanding, and even compassion, develop for the person suffering from the abusive personality. We use the word "suffering" intentionally. Remember that an abuser was first someone else's victim. Bear in mind also that within every victim is the seed for abuse. Statistics illustrate that 97.5% of all battering parents were battered children.

Based on these truths, abusers seem to be victims who have crossed an invisible line. They are expressing the effects of the abuse on their own personalities. They seem to believe that in order to take control of their own lives, to avoid being further victimized by anyone, they must become aggressive themselves. It is not that they wake up one morning and decide to cause someone else the same degree of pain they have received, not even to get even. Nor do they reason that if they are aggressive enough toward others, they themselves will never be abused again. They are acting out of the deep pain they feel. Their actions are reactions to internal driving forces, which are usually evil spirits. Most of the time, their own hurts, wounds, and damaged self-images force them to do the very things they have endured. They may have even sworn that they would NEVER hurt anyone as they were hurt. But as the pressures build up, the abusers strike out to alleviate their own internal stresses. The principle is similar to that of a pressure valve. As the water heats and the boiling action begins, in order to safely alleviate the building pressure, the valve releases steam.

Abusers seldom understand why they react as they do. Like so many victims, they fight problems with lapses of memory. In fact, the most difficult to work with are abusers who are in full control of their memories, yet still inflict pain on others! The most difficult to stir up ANY sympathy for are those perpetrators of abuse directed at children, or the elderly, or a woman we know to be defenseless or easily hurt. There are at least seven other reasons why ministering to abusers is so difficult.

1. If you are working with the victim, your emotions can become so involved that the abuser becomes YOUR enemy also!

2. If you have an abuser on your staff, or in some other way the abuse affects you directly:

a. The result of the abuse makes your job more difficult, painful, or fearful.

b. The attacks undermine your authority and hinder your effectiveness.

c. The abuser stirs up strife, adding more problems for you to solve.

d. You are then forced to observe others under you being hurt unnecessarily.

3. If the abuser behaves in such a manner as to become the villain, he makes himself difficult to defend.

4. If there seems to be no logical reason for the attacks, the abuser is seen as one whose motivating force is dominance and control, at any cost, regardless of any hurt inflicted.

5. If the abuser portrays an attitude of superiority,

intimidation, unteachableness, arrogance, or unrepentance, you think he is saying, "I have done nothing wrong, mind your own business!"

6. If your feelings toward the abuser are totally negative, it is a natural reaction to his actions.

7. If the abuser requires more time and ministry than his victim, remember that basically he is also a victim. Because he has chosen to inflict abuse on someone else to express his own hurt, he requires added ministry.

The abusive personality is one of the most confusing and internally chaotic of all. The abuser has the same weakness and fears that torment his victim. That is to say, the abuser is tormented by the same evil spirits that torment his prey. Therefore, in dealing with him, you may behold a fragile victim one minute, and the next minute meet an aggressive, violent abuser releasing his pent-up anger. He may strike out with an attitude of dominance, criticism, and control. Can there be two spirits with such opposite assignments present? The answer is a definite YES.

After abuse has taken hold and become his pattern, the abuser is held in bondage to a cycle of behavior. Complex and intricate intercommunication develops between the abuser and his victim, understood only by the two of them. There are five threads which cause this interweaving process:

1. Shared guilt.
2. Shared shame.
3. Mutual fear of exposure.
4. A need to alter reality in order to protect himself and justify his behavior and his reactions.
5. The existence of a spiritual bond between himself and the victim.

The last thread is the primary key to the complete release of the abuser! These spiritual bonds MUST be broken. The abuser must first forgive his own abusers, then forgive himself for the abuse he has committed. After that the spirit and power of his own abuser over him must be broken, then his own spirit and power over his victim broken. The abuser MUST right the situation between himself and his victim; then he absolutely MUST repair his relationship with God.

Unless BOTH relationships have been made right, the abuser will continue to suffer. The psychological effect of the abuse he perpetrated will cause continuing emotional strain and problems with coping mechanisms.

In some cases, the abuse has been going on since the abuser was an adolescent. This is especially true if the nature of the abuse was sexual. The emotional torment of the abuser seems to have its root in buried guilt, which is not difficult to understand. The Bible states in definite words that unconfessed sin produces guilt, and that it then gives place to the destructive power of condemnation. Under any unconfessed sin, man always reverts back to his responses in the Garden of Eden, as recorded in Genesis 3.

1. Man became overwhelmed by the cost of sin and the destruction that sin causes. In verse 7 of chapter 3, Adam and Eve's eyes were opened, and they realized that the cost of their sin was to have lost the covering of God's holiness.

2. Man was then forced into efforts to cover himself with the dead systems that the world used to justify its actions. In verse 7, Adam and Eve covered themselves with material that would have to be replaced regularly.

3. Worldly methods provided neither freedom nor forgiveness. Hence, Satan could further cripple man with unrelenting shame that produced fear and separation from God. In verse 8, Adam and Eve were hiding from the only One who could restore, heal, and renew.

4. Man's shame caused greater fear of God's presence, and avoidance of God's correction. In verse 11, God

directly questioned Adam about the cause of his fear and hiding, only to have Adam avoid a direct answer. God knew that the key to forgiveness and new life was in honest confession of sin.

5. Avoided repentance clouded their ability to admit their own guilt, confess their sin, and receive forgiveness for their actions. In verse 12, Adam said, in effect, "Look, God, this is really all Your fault. It was Your idea to give me this woman in the first place!"

6. Delayed repentance produced hardness of heart and denial of responsibility, allowing Adam to blame everyone else for his sins and resulting problems. In verse 11, after his attempt to blame God would not fly, Adam blamed Eve, who in turn said, "Who, me? Not me, the serpent is at fault!"

7. Repression of guilt, and avoidance of dealing with sin, cause the loss of personal peace, and freedom from the effects of sin. In verses 14-24, God had no choice but to judge the sin, invoke the curse, and drive them from the Garden.

The personality of the abuser is formed by being severely damaged and never having received healing. His reactions are thus based on fear and low self-esteem. He has lost all confidence in his own ability to accomplish anything of value. He seems to believe that his only hope for respect, authority, or control is through intimidation or force. Addictions and compulsions put more pressure on him so that he feels even less in control of himself. The abuser's hatred for himself was caused by his own early mistreatment, but he needs someone to blame NOW and hold responsible for his own failures. He does not cope well with pressure, but is so afraid of failing that he cannot admit to making mistakes. Obviously, he is very insecure and fears being exposed as the failure he is SURE that he is. With such a pitiful self-image, you can see that he needs to feel superior to someone! With enough amnesia to have no memories of the incidents that caused such damage to his personality, he is as driven by shadows as is his victim.

Most abusers are not only in need of someone to abuse, but they need to receive abuse periodically. If they cannot arrange for an outside abuser, they will become their own. They will set themselves up to fail by working to destroy any relationships established on a positive basis. They put a stop to potentially positive experiences, even going so far as to avoid receiving awards or honors they have worked to achieve. In an attempt to arrange for an outside abuser, they will find an authority figure to cast in that role. The abuser instinctively knows how to manipulate this authority figure into becoming his stand-in abuser. This has some interesting side effects, especially if that leader is neither a victim nor an abuser. He comes under such guilt that he can no longer minister to the abuser effectively. He begins to question his own motives, and may become a less effective minister himself. He may come to believe that there is something evil within himself! He forms an aversion to any and all abusers.

Meanwhile, our abuser has altered his perception of any situation where he was receiving help. Because he accepts only the negatives, he feels justified in depriving himself of the benefit of any help. Simultaneously, he produces his own pain of separation, deprivation of positive affirmation, and being hurt by another person. Of course, all this occurs at the subconscious level. The abuser is not aware that he has distorted anything! Nor is he aware of any need to suffer. Remember that the abuser was and is a victim himself, and therefore develops as much internal turmoil in the face of success as does a victim.

Eventually, the abuser (again unconsciously) may begin to arrange for the abuse he is inflicting to be exposed to someone in a position of legal, family, or spiritual authority. Once the abuse is exposed, the abuser seems to work extra hard to deny that it ever occurred. This denial stage seems to provide tremendous reinforcement to his personality. Not only does he get an adrenalin high from convincing everyone that he is innocent, but he gets a false sense of security and of innocence by escaping blame.

Many professionals who frequently work with abusers believe that if an abuser manages to regularly and successfully complete this exposure/innocence cycle, he can continue to avoid reality indefinitely. Other professional counselors believe that the abuser honestly accepts his own behavior as good, and beyond challenging. (If this be so, it is easy to see why a deceiving spirit is so often found with an abuser!) The abuser's success in completing this cycle does give the impression that he is not seriously interested in help. While not necessarily true, it certainly is one of his best defense mechanisms for keeping people at arm's length. His success also produces a feeling that he has made fools of those who have been trying to help him. Consequently, on their next attempt to help the abuser, they will be full of suspicion and extra caution, which may well hinder their effectiveness.

As was delineated in the chapter on spouse abuse, abuse is extremely cyclical, and therefore easily charted and observed. It has distinct patterns which announce the point at which the abuser is more open to receiving help and admitting his problem. What should always be kept in mind is that as the abuser experiences more frustration and internal pain, the cycle repeats itself more frequently. The cycle takes less and less time to complete, thereby intensifying the abuser's desperate need to be shown that the power and love of God are as much for him as for his victim. The love, forgiveness, and freedom which God desires to minister to the abuser is difficult for those ministering to demonstrate, unless God reveals to them His love for the abuser.

NOTE: Compassion can only be received by seeing the abuser as God does. Otherwise, the initial reaction of hostility will be sensed by the abuser and he will cover as much of the problem as he possibly can. Thereafter he will be trapped in his belief that there IS no help for him, in God or anywhere else!

Since the abuser was also a victim of some form of abuse before he became an abuser, it is not uncommon for him to take on the appearance outlined in the chapters on physical and sexual abuse. However, in some cases the mode of dress will express the macho image, or the image of rigid control. If the expression is in the macho vein, both male and female will go out of their way to dress in a manner that will emphasize physical strength and the strength of their personality. The body language says, "I am the boss here."

If, instead, the vein is rigid control, the clothing will be restrictive and will not lend itself to free-flowing movement. The body language now informs everyone that he is up-tight and restrained. Sometimes he gives the impression of either a volcano ready to erupt, or an iceberg that will never thaw.

The primary goal in dealing with an abuser should be to use these tools to ask the right questions with enough love and conviction to force the abuser to admit his intense need for help. Unless he will confess his problem and honestly desire to change his life, the abuser (more than any other personality) will never gain freedom. The main reason is because he holds so many other lives in his grasp. He gains a false sense of power through controlling the lives of others.

When ministering to the abuser, follow the patterns delineated in the chapter dealing with the specific type or types of abuse he originally suffered. Then begin to look for some of the following spirits, and allow the Holy Spirit to reveal others to you:

1. Abuse.
2. Violence.
3. Anger, hate, rage, hostility, murder.
4. Dominance and control, manipulation.
5. Fear of exposure.
6. Deception, false reality, lying.
7. Perfection.

8. Unforgiveness, of themselves and others, and sometimes even of God.
9. Torment.
10. Bitterness, resentment, self-hate.
11. Hopelessness, helplessness, despair.
12. Amnesia.
13. Self-righteousness.
14. Strife and contention.
15. Rejection.

Chapter 14

FEAR

Fear has become modern man's constant companion. The more complex and high-tech our society becomes, the more man is harassed by fears of all types. As the family unit deteriorates, as technology and pollution threaten our environment, and as catastrophic illnesses arrest our attention, man feels that he is completely out of control of his life, his future and his health. Such a state paves the way for fears to progress to the levels of phobias. We now have more types of diagnosed phobic personalities than ever in the history of man.

This problem is as troubling to the body of Jesus Christ as it is to the secular world. The increase of violence and abuse in the home has greatly contributed to the problem of fear in children, affecting the healthy formation of personalities. Since fear has become a widespread problem, it is critical to a healthy body of Christ that those in a position of leadership and ministry be trained to recognize the symptoms of the phobic personality, and detect fear as the root cause of the symptoms. They must minister God's freedom and His healing from the effects of fear.

This need is heightened because current thinking believes that fear, now a common foe, should no longer be considered a personality disorder in its less severe stages, but is merely the result of a complex, competitive, affluent and technological culture. This line of thought also assumes that every successful person with a reasonable IQ and intact self-image should be able to form coping and repressive skills to deal with the internal turmoil produced by fear, without seeking outside help. These erroneous conclusions have prevented many in the secular world from receiving help. Few are willing to admit to weakness. In fact, it seems that, by today's thinking, the more a problem becomes the expression of the norm, the less it should be taken seriously by the church.

Satan is beginning to infiltrate the church with this logic, so that he can be free to destroy and imprison more people than ever before! He knows the makeup of the carnal nature so well that he understands the most effective way to paralyze and sidetrack the church. He will attempt to convince us that since the problem is so widespread, we would be foolish to believe it has a spiritual cause and is a result of the first sins. He is, in fact, convincing the church that we will appear primitive and superstitious and that no one will take us seriously if we continue to expose and deal with fear. This leaves him totally unchecked to be exactly what he is—the proverbial "weasel in the hen house"!

The body of Christ should be shouting, "Wake up!" There is hope, freedom and healing from the roots that produce fear. Sadly enough, the truth is that fear has ravaged the world, the church, and the ministry itself. Therefore, this book would provide no real service if we did not address those areas of fear underlying the current behavior of the body of Christ.

Our problem is that it is often difficult to unmask the root of fear in the church, because to admit to fear is considered unspiritual and lacking in even elementary levels of faith. Listed below are some ways the root of fear affects the functions of the body:

1. FEAR is one of the most effective weapons of destruction Satan has aimed against mankind since the Garden of Eden.

2. FEAR is one of the greatest hindrances to man's living an abundant life: a life filled with confidence in God's nature, and the knowledge that God's plans and purposes are good, not evil.

3. FEAR and distrust of God were results of the first sin, and hence are a part of the curse we live under today. They are also the most effective weapons Satan has for keeping people from forming that initial relationship with Jesus Christ.

4. FEAR is the most universal emotion experienced by man. It can either impede or halt spiritual, mental and social growth. It affects relationships, professional accomplishment, creativity, and healthy perspectives.

5. FEAR, which masquerades itself as shyness, is exposed and broken in prayer and under God's anointing.

6. FEAR forces people to avoid confronting issues, situations and individuals, even though they know that confrontation would bring freedom from misunderstanding, and would reestablish unity and loving relationships.

7. FEAR produces a compulsion to perfection. If spiritual people are supposed to be able to receive direction from God, it is assumed that the direction will work out perfectly without any hitches. Should something not work out, the person's spirituality is called into question.

8. FEAR hinders those in the body of Christ, including those in ministry, by causing them to doubt that they hear God. This doubt keeps Christians unstable enough to keep them tenuous and of no real threat.

9. FEAR produces severe anxiety over whether God will trust us with greater responsibility, particularly if we believe we cannot hear Him.

10. FEAR causes severe struggles with feelings of inadequacy and inferiority, which eventually prevent the release of all our gifts and talents.

11. FEAR causes jealousy, competition, mistrust, the questioning of motives, and the "I am going to build my own Kingdom" mentality.

12. FEAR produces a distorted view of God which

convinces us that His standards and ministry requirements are too high to attain.

13. FEAR then succeeds in putting a distance between us and God, preventing an intimate love relationship with Him.

14. FEAR induces a perverted "fear of God," convincing us that we have become His slaves, rather than His empowered sons, with all the benefits of His Kingdom within our reach. Like the Prodigal Son, we waste years eating the husks rather than doing the business of the Family, wearing His rings, His robes, and His shoes.

15. FEAR keeps more people in bondage than any other spirit. It robs them of the ability to reach out and receive God's freedom, by convincing them that something terrible, embarrassing, or harmful will happen to them during ministry.

Why is it so important to lull the church to sleep and keep it from dealing with the root causes of fear? Satan KNOWS and TREMBLES at what we in the body of Christ do not seem to comprehend. The power possessed by the church through the blood of Jesus Christ will bring complete peace and freedom to a fearful heart.

We seem to have forgotten how often Jesus addressed an individual in trouble, in need of healing or deliverance, or involved in a supernatural encounter with God, with the one word "peace." The full meaning of this word is "freedom from all the effects of sin." How Satan must tremble, to think that the church could rise up to take her God-given authority, and dispel and expose fear for what it truly is—one of the effects of sin.

Remember, church, that God said 365 times, *"Be not afraid,"* or used one of its derivatives. One "fear not" for every day of the year! Further, consider that just before Jesus was about to be crucified, He admonished His disciples in John 14:27:

Peace I leave with you, My peace I give unto you: not

as the world giveth, give I unto you. Let not your heart be troubled, neither let it be afraid.

We can believe, from the command at the end of that verse, that Jesus is ordering us to go on the offensive against fear. This verse should both excite and encourage us, as it makes plain that we have the power and authority to drive fear from our hearts. Then we are not subject to the wiles of Satan to paralyze us with fear; we CAN do something to overcome him!

For those in positions of leadership or ministry responsibility, it is imperative, for the following reasons, to recognize the manifestations of a fearful personality.

1. FEAR paralyzes our ability to make decisions.
2. FEAR causes us to react rather than act.
3. FEAR produces a tendency to withdraw to:
   a. A place perceived to be safe and free from harm.
   b. A false mental state that represses consideration of the problem inducing fear.
   c. A situation of safety where duties and responsibilities can be performed without fear of exposure or negative evaluation.
   d. Situations surrounded by people we perceive as non-threatening.
4. FEAR keeps us from being stretched or made vulnerable. We are hindered from reaching our full potential.
5. FEAR causes us to become uncomfortable, embarrassed, or so self-conscious that we become hostile and defensive. (This does great damage, since groups only make as much progress as there is unity and mutual trust.)
6. FEAR induces us to erect high walls of protection around ourselves. Therefore, healthy interaction is impossible and we do not learn how to receive or give love. (This prevents us from understanding or accepting the love of God, despite the number of times we are told of it.)

7. FEAR produces in us a compulsive refusal to admit any mistakes or misjudgments.

8. FEAR forces us into a defensive stance, resulting in both recalcitrance and an unwillingness to be taught.

9. FEAR keeps us from all types of confrontation, thereby limiting our success levels.

10. FEAR imprisons us behind the bars of anxiety, regarding invisible enemies and projected problems that never materialize.

11. FEAR imposes on us a personality described as inferior and insecure.

12. FEAR binds us into functioning far below our capabilities, because it puts a stop to normal daily routines. Fear alters our ability to travel, get near water, cross bridges, ride elevators or escalators, be near people, be in close or wide-open spaces or extreme heights, or speak before groups.

A phobic personality is not formed by one or two events. Phobia is a progressive problem; therefore one type of fear leads into the next. In most cases, the affected individuals have no conscious memory of the cause of the consuming fear. Interestingly enough, when the root causes are of a totally spiritual nature, there is no environmental or experiential reason for the fear. To complicate the situation, those people gripped by fear feel so hopeless, frustrated and abnormal that they are incapable of asking for help. They compensate for their fears as long as they can. This is one of the hardest responses to understand, primarily because the phobic personalities are more intensely afraid of the ability of the professional to incarcerate, institutionalize, or humiliate them by holding them up to public scorn.

It must be further pointed out that our children are taught (sometimes by very embarrassing methods, particularly if they are boys) that fear is a very weak and sissy emotion. We drill into their heads that there is nothing to fear, and that if they are afraid it is because their imaginations are playing tricks on them. Some parents make their children feel like they are complete failures if they require night lights. We are guilty today of a worship of machismo at all costs. Our movie and television heroes are rough, aggressive and intimidating. Seldom is the male lead a mild-mannered, easygoing person. As a result of such programming and public standards, those fighting the losing battle against fear feel ashamed and inferior to the rest of society.

In the beginning stages of the problem, the person usually knows how to cover any outward symptoms, or to withdraw from situations that trigger the fear, long before their behavior would give them away. Those in the early stages of fear, and those in a more advanced stage of the phobia, are so in control of their logical reasoning faculties that they have full awareness of everything that is happening. It is as though they are mere observers watching events being played out on a stage over which they have no control.

In most cases, symptoms that can be observed in the early stages of fear are:

1. Restlessness that cannot be easily contained.
2. A stillness that makes the rest of the group extremely uncomfortable.
3. Low level of self-esteem.
4. Need for constant reinforcement.
5. Body language that portrays an arrogance and self-conceit that keeps everyone at arm's length.
6. Excessive movement of the hands.
7. Sweaty palms, even though they are very still.
8. Nervous laughter or inappropriate expressions of laughter.
9. A silence that implies, "I find all of this beneath my need to respond or get involved."
10. A compulsion to dominate the conversation of the group, stemming from a need to protect themselves from evaluation by the group.

11. A need to hide in the group, giving the nonverbal communication, "I am not here and, more importantly, neither do I want to be."

12. A wide territorial space.

13. Darting eyes that observe every change in their environment.

14. Tremendous apprehension when unable to observe every entrance and exit in the room.

15. A need to excessively touch everyone they communicate with to gain reassurance and approval.

16. A flushed appearance that may be described as splotchy.

17. An extremely pale complexion that looks pasty.

Apart from the fearful and phobic persons who develop as a result of other personality problems, there are other phobias. These stem from a traumatic event, or are the result of inherited spirits.

A very simple definition of PHOBIA is: fear that has progressed to an irrational level. Its victims usually realize its irrationality, but are helpless to halt its control over their lives. The definition alone is a clue that the cause has a spiritual root. Behavior gone wild, totally out of the individual's control with no apparent cause, bears Satan's signature in capital letters!

The above definition indicates that a phobic personality brings a series of different problems into a group. Fear is as contagious as rebellion. Phobic individuals function at levels of desperate awareness of their problems and how irrational they seem to all observers. Realizing how ridiculous they seem, they build defense mechanisms that push others away before they can be hurt or be made the brunt of a joke. They are controlled by something they do not understand. The resulting levels of frustration make fearful persons difficult to relate to.

It should be noted that one of the first blocks that may be faced in offering freedom to phobic individuals is that in their unconscious minds there are benefits to the phobias. They may have difficulty releasing their problems until they sincerely hate the effects. Among the supposed benefits are that the phobia is a defense mechanism. Unconsciously, they do not trust themselves to control their dangerous impulses. It also serves as a release from internal stresses they cannot satisfactorily handle. Actually, the phobia covers the root fear. For example, suppose a man has developed a fear of being terminated from his job because its demands are above his capabilities. It is necessary for him to cross several bridges en route to work. The fear of termination is transferred to a fear of bridges, thus enabling him to quit the job and never expose his root fear of inadequacy. It is imperative that, as you minister to this person, the true problem be exposed by your questions. Fears so intense as to be phobic increase attention, sympathy, assistance, and control over people and situations. The victim can now be free from experiencing unpleasant situations that could show up his weaknesses or force him to begin to take on the responsbilities of wholeness.

The next few sections will scan some of the more common phobias and delineate some of the more obvious symptoms.

One of the most common phobias is a FEAR OF WATER. Once an individual, though unconsciously, has allowed fear to progress to a phobia, the door opens for Satan to plant related spirits of fear. These fears may have stemmed from traumatic events, or events perceived by the child as traumatic. The sequence often begins with fear of a large standing body of water, usually the swimming pool, and then, as it takes more control, it progresses to include rivers, streams, lakes, ponds and the ocean. As this fear dominates the person, he becomes afraid of bridges, boats and even bathtubs. The fear manifests itself by causing such a severe anxiety attack that the person begins to experience sweaty palms, paralyzed thought processes, hyperventilation, or extreme nausea. There may also be a loss of the conscious ability to take action, but not the loss of body function or operation. In fact, many perform actions that override the fear while in an almost trance-like state.

This phobia manifests itself as follows: When driving a car and approaching a bridge, they will often either freeze and be totally unable to cross the bridge, or they will lose the awareness of their surroundings. They will stay frozen until something jars them (horns, people). Most often at that point they will turn their car around and seek an alternative route. If they are the passengers, the panic becomes so severe they lose control and their behavior reaches intense levels of emotion. They may even demand to leave the car and walk over. This presents another problem, however, as they will only get partially across the bridge and freeze, unable to go forward or backward.

The fear of water is closely associated at times with fear of drowning and fear of death. It can develop from having been thrown into a swimming pool while a small child, in an attempt to force him to swim.

As the problem intensifies, the individuals unwittingly open the door to even more oppressive problems. For example, they now develop fears of enclosed and close spaces if forced onto a boat. This progresses to the point where the person is now fighting a battle with claustrophobia too.

CLAUSTROPHOBIA afflicts a growing number of people as violence and other stresses of a highly urban society take over our lives. This fear consists of a combination of fears: of tight spaces, fear of the dark, of small places, and fear of crowded places. Claustrophobia usually operates when the persons are alone, but can surface in what they perceive as a crowded place with no adequate exit.

The symptoms will again include intense anxiety, causing sweaty palms, paralyzed thought processes, panic attacks, hyperventilation, and nausea. Added to these physical symptoms will usually be demands for a wide territorial space, and an inability to wear tight, restrictive clothing, especially if it has to be pulled on over their heads. They will be unable to ride in elevators, especially if there are other people aboard, and unable to close the doors of phone booths. Only with great difficulty will they be able to stand in long lines that have restrictive barriers. They will not allow themselves to be placed at a table in which they feel cornered, nor will they use crowded mass transportation.

As this fear progresses, its victims again open doors to other problems and become afraid of crowds, afraid of being abandoned, and afraid of the dark. They become even more incapable of living full, normal lives. Shopping in grocery stores with narrow aisles becomes impossible; shopping for clothes becomes complicated as they cannot use a dressing room that is enclosed; and driving their car in peak traffic hours causes intense panic: they feel hedged in and fight the urge to get out and run. They deteriorate to the point that often even basement stairs become a trial to negotiate, or a walk-in closet an overwhelming barrier to getting dressed.

Claustrophobia seems to have its roots in being abused as a child, the occurrence of a traumatic event, or in a play situation that got out of hand. For example, perhaps a child, as punishment or as abuse, was locked up in a small, dark place and then left there for a period of time. Another example could be a difficult labor that caused the baby a near-death trauma. An abnormally long period in the birth canal could also be a root cause. Claustrophobia can also stem from the fear resulting from a child being smothered, as an expression of abuse, or in a play situation where the child is repeatedly tickled to the point of losing his breath. It could be brought on by being involved in an accident where one was trapped for a long time. Claustrophobia can be induced in adulthood by the very same causes and seems to progress at a more rapid rate if it indeed enters in adulthood.

A phobia that is currently drawing a great deal of media attention is AGORAPHOBIA. Agoraphobia can be best defined as a fear of open spaces. People who suffer from this phobia have at their disposal a large number of support groups to help them recover. There are counselors and therapists who have so specialized in this phobia that they are willing to make house calls. There are many theories about the root cause of agoraphobia. Unfortunately, more is unknown about this problem than is known. The onset seems to be sudden and without obvious reason. It is intertwined with several other phobias, which may explain its sudden appearance in the lives of its victims. Some state that they are fine one day and are experiencing symptoms the very next day.

The phobias intertwined with agoraphobia are fear of people, fear of comparison, fear of people's faces, and fear of self. At this stage victims no longer trust their own reactions or ability to function normally. Early symptoms are the usual ones for any fear. Their onset occurs when the individuals are forced to enter environments they do not perceive as safe. Oddly enough, the first panic attack often occurs while driving a car. They suddenly become overwhelmed with an urge to return home. If they do not immediately do so, they begin to experience the usual fearful reactions.

An interesting pattern can occur in these cases. If the individuals give in to the panic, the likelihood is that they will never be capable of driving alone again. Conversely, if they successfully fight and overcome the first occurrence of physical reaction, they will still be subject to waves of nausea at the very thought of driving anywhere alone. As a result, they seek the company of an intimidating authority figure whom they believe to be dependable. When it was observed that the first thing the individuals did was seek out an intimidating authority figure, it was thought that possibly agoraphobia has its root in a damaged personality. The phobic individuals are usually drawn to an authority figure who, for his own needs, wants to keep them dependent.

Untreated and without ministry, the length of this

stage depends on the victims and their ability to fight. The condition can continue to deteriorate until the agoraphobic victims cannot function normally, even with the authority figure. At this point, the symptoms will include dizziness, a tendency to black out, and paranoia. They may hear voices, telling them that there are people out in those open spaces, waiting to hurt them.

The next stage finds agoraphobics incapable of entering any open spaces at any time in the company of anyone. They even stop being able to visit family and friends they know well and should not find threatening. If the pattern of retreat is not checked, the individuals become incapable of leaving home. In its ultimate stage, they will be incapable of coming out of one room where they feel safe, nor will they be able to let anyone enter. The symptoms at this stage include voices that tell them they will make a scene if they go outside. They may suffer hysteria that may cause them to run in blind panic, or cause them to freeze and be incapable of movement. Some try to inflict physical pain on themselves, hoping to eliminate the mental anguish. Such extreme fears have been attributed to mental torture, where one is berated continuously, or the end of (or change in) a dependent relationship.

The most recent phobia to demand media attention is the SUDDEN PANIC SYNDROME, or as it is now more commonly being referred to, S.P.S. As our society morals and mores continue to change and become more complicated, so do the fears and phobias we suffer. An interesting correlation is that the symptoms of these two present-day phobias (agoraphobia and S.P.S.) seem to be more devastating and more difficult to trace to their root causes. An observation of note is that S.P.S. became more frequent when therapists and counselors were becoming more confident in the progress being made with the treatment of agoraphobia. Could it be that we are observing the beginning of the fulfillment of one of the signs listed in Luke 21:25-36? In verse 26, we read:

Men's hearts failing them for fear, and for looking

after those things which are coming on the earth: for the powers of heaven shall be shaken.

Presently S.P.S. is being diagnosed as a genetic disorder that floods the body with a hundred times the adrenalin needed during times of severe trauma. Since it is genetic, it is being considered incurable. However, its symptoms can be treated with medication. One of the most confusing elements of this disorder is that it can go into remission for years, only to reappear without warning or apparent cause. There seems to be no clear agreement as to what induces the remission.

S.P.S. is a two-fold disorder consisting of panic and phobia. The four most common symptoms of panic are:

1. Hyperventilation, at which point the S.P.S. sufferer feels unable to breathe at all.
2. Sensations of having a heart attack, including the feeling that he is dying.
3. Shaking and trembling.
4. Clammy palms.

The five most common symptoms of phobia associated with S.P.S. are:

1. The development of overwhelming fears that vary with each sufferer, but always serve to curtail, then eliminate, their activities.
2. Listlessness that intensifies as new fears continue to be added.
3. Withdrawal from society, friends, and family as the disorder intensifies, because the attacks come without warning.
4. Possible development of these fears into paranoia.
5. Developing a knowing that they are no longer normal.

Since so much of the S.P.S. disorder is still uncertain and shrouded with mystery, it would behoove you to consider spiritual causes. When ministering to one with S.P.S., the interweaving between panic and phobias must not be ignored. Therefore, the spirits usually found in panic are hysteria, apprehension, dread, worry, and anxiety. These must be eliminated in addition to those associated with each individual phobia the victim suffers. It might further be well to ascertain from the Holy Spirit if also present are those spirits found in compulsive and addictive personalities, especially those involved in adrenalin addiction.

Another fear prevalent today is FEAR OF THE DARK. These people are truly incapable of entering a dark room, sleeping in the dark, walking outside at night, or driving alone at night, and have deep-seated fears of being attacked. The symptoms are:

1. When they walk down a dark street or hall, they experience a rush of adrenalin.
2. Their sleep patterns are restless and they sleep in short intervals, beginning at the first sign of dawn.
3. They will imagine monsters in their rooms, in their closets, or under their beds.
4. They are prone to nightmares.
5. They will awaken with severe anxiety attacks.
6. When they are out at night, they will imagine that they hear someone behind them.
7. When driving, they feel the presence of someone in their car ready to do them harm.
8. They often must fight a powerful urge to pull off the road.

Additional symptoms are covered in greater detail in the chapters dealing with the different forms of abuse.

God realized that fear, in one form or another, would be a catalyst to drive man into sin. He always acknowledged its existence and provided, in the power of forgiveness, freedom from the destruction of fear. God, knowing well man's nature, understood that fear would also arise when He revealed Himself in a supernatural manner. Graciously, He provided peace and an answer to this fear in His very nature. In Judges 6:24 we see God's provision as He reveals Himself as Jehovah during an encounter with Gideon. In Abraham's life, God revealed His character and His nature by changing His name to establish the foundation of Abraham's faith. Therefore, it should not surprise us to find God dealing early on with this problem of fear. In Genesis 15:1, God changed His name to Jehovah Magon and said,

> . . . *Fear not, Abram: I am thy shield, and thy exceeding great reward.*

The word picture is one of an individually crafted shield that extended from the neck to below the knees, and wrapped almost completely around the warrior. God seemed to be saying, "I have you covered."

Throughout the Gospels, Jesus said, "Fear not." Fear drove Elijah into the desert for a forty-day journey to escape one woman whom Satan had built up in his mind to superhuman proportions. If we can establish the truth of Genesis 15:1 in our spirits, and in the spirits of those to whom we minister, Satan will have lost his biggest key for keeping people enslaved by fear.

When ministering to those with intense fears, begin by giving them a Scriptural basis to reestablish their faith. There is no prison too big for God to deliver His children from safely, and nothing too hard for God to handle!

Then establish as fact that their fears do not embarrass God, catch Him off guard, or find Him unprepared to handle them. Begin to unearth the origin of their fears. Do they result from one of the other personalities mentioned in this book, or is fear really the root problem? Isolate the main fear and proceed to eliminate its possible causes, whether natural or spiritual. Remember to determine whether or not they are now absolutely ready to live free from fear, to operate at normal levels of productivity and responsibility.

Some of the spirits that may be present, in addition to those directly pertaining to the individual fears, are:

1. King of terrors.
2. Fear of memories, of remembering traumatic experiences.
3. Fear of exposure.
4. Fear of the past.
5. Fear of rejection.
6. Fear of pain.
7. Fear of being ridiculed.
8. Fear of failure.
9. Fear of being abandoned.
10. Fear of being unloved and unaccepted.
11. Fear of success.
12. Fear of God and His ways.

To state the obvious, one who is extremely afraid to go near water has a spirit of fear. So you see that specific spirits of fear found in each of the individual phobias often reveal their names by their actions.

Chapter 15

AFTERCARE

Everyone wants quick answers to every question and immediate solutions to every problem. Unfortunately, life has more complexity than we care to deal with. Most people have accumulated years of problem living before they seek any kind of help, or indeed find anyone who can offer real assistance. Most secular therapists regard man as a two-part being, body and soul. God made us a three-part being, spirit, soul and body. If we ignore the spiritual dimension, we are as the proverbial ostrich with our head in the sand. We are programmed by our genes to grow physically to maturity. Diet and nutrition alter what nature intends. If the body is deprived of protein or critical minerals during the growth phases, serious and permanent effects will result. The same is true of our emotional development. If a child is deprived of nurturing care, the consequences are indelibly registered on the personality. It cannot be overemphasized that loving, nurturing care must begin soon after conception, and continue to maturity.

We give undernourished people therapeutic doses of vitamins and minerals in an attempt to overcome the effects of deprivation. At times these measures are indeed beneficial, but, alas, it is not one hundred percent effective and we can only hope to minimize damage and prevent further negative effects. So also, we can lavish attention on the unloved, the unwanted, the downtrodden and the abused, but, in like manner, there may be too little too late.

We must keep in mind that with God all things are possible, and that the effectual fervent prayers of the righteous avail much. What may be an impossible case to the world will be a small thing for the Lord. We must endure with patience, as the husbandman, waiting for the precious fruit. We must never give up hope. We have seen remarkable transformations in the attitude, personality and self-esteem of numerous individuals. We have seen the power of God set people free from a lifetime of demonic bondage within minutes, bondage that years of therapy and counseling never touched. Jesus indeed came to set at liberty those that are bound, to let the oppressed go free.

Once free, there is a period of time when new thought patterns will be developed, and old habits will have to be replaced with new ones. As a medical patient needs a time of recuperation, physical therapy and follow-up care, so also do the casualties and victims of Satan's destruction. There is always a danger that the one set free will move too quickly into areas where he is not strong enough to withstand the attacks and counter-attacts of the enemy. God warned the Children of Israel that He would not give them all of the land in one year, " . . . lest the land become desolate and the beast of the field multiply against thee. By little and little I will drive them out from before thee, until thou be increased, and inherit the land" (Exodus 23:29-30).

In III John 1:2 we read:

"Beloved, I wish above all things that thou mayest prosper and be in health, even as thy soul prospereth."

And we are again reminded of the connection between the psuche (soul) and the soma (body). As the soul prospers, the body enjoys health. Wholeness is the objective, in body, soul and spirit. While the secular world focuses on the "body," the real basis for prosperity and health is in the realm of the spirit. Violation of God's laws has inevitable consequences. Regardless of what the secular world says, sin is sin and *"the soul that sinneth, it shall die."* No matter what man may do to change a truth into a lie, the spirit of man knows that the person is sinning, and this brings guilt, which begins to have its effect on the soul, which in turn causes reactions in the body.

For true bodily health, the person must be reconciled to God, all sins confessed and repented of and the person walking in obedience to the Word of God. Persistent sin will ultimately cause sickness in soul and body. AIDS is not caused by a virus, it is caused by sin. Stop the sin, and the disease will cease. The virus is the consequence of sin. Sin opens the door for both physical and spiritual infection. A body weakened in its natural defenses can be attacked by bacteria, viruses and fungi. A soul that is devoid of spiritual strength will fall easy prey to the evil spirits that inhabit our society.

In the fifth chapter of the Gospel of John, after Jesus healed the man at the pool of Bethesda, Jesus told him to *". . . sin no more, lest a worse thing come unto thee."* The verb tense is to "stop continuing to sin." The inference is clear that continuing sin has opened the door and "something" has come unto the man and Jesus has just released him from it. Continuing to sin will allow something worse to "come unto" him. In Luke 11:24-25 Jesus tells us that when the spirit is gone out of a man, it will try to return and re-enter, bringing others that are more wicked than itself, and the last state of the person is worse than the first. It is important that the person freed of unclean spirits walk in righteousness and avoid his old sinful ways, keeping the "house" (body and soul) filled up with wholesome and clean things.

Proverbs 23:7 states, *"For as a man thinketh in his heart, so is he."* II Corinthians 10:4 tells us that we are to bring every thought into captivity to the obedience of Christ. We are responsible for our thought life. The battle rages in the mind. What we meditate on will control us. We are commanded to meditate on the Word of God day and night. Thinking unclean thoughts, coveting, scheming, remembering and reliving old wounds will cause a root of bitterness to spring up and bear gall and wormwood.

Ministry to the oppressed is not a "one-shot" deal. There has to be a commitment to follow through and nurture the victim back to health. Remember, the parable of the Good Samaritan is our example. Jesus pours in the oil and the wine, but we are the innkeeper and we are to tend the wounded until they recover, and when Jesus returns He will repay us whatever we have spent.

Consider a young sapling that is bent over and tied down to a stake driven into the ground. This is an unnatural condition, and if the young tree is left in this condition for a long period, there will be serious consequences. After months or years of being "bound" to the stake, changes will occur in the direction of the branches as they grow "upward" to catch the sunlight. The branches on the lower side will wither and possibly die from lack of light. The result is an abnormal tree. Now suppose that someone comes along and sees the situation and decides to cut the tree free of the binding rope. Does the tree snap upright and suddenly take on a normal shape? Of course not!

Why should we expect people who have been bound for years with chains of darkness suddenly to be whole and normal after one ministry session? After the tree is released, there must be a careful pushing and propping of the trunk to straighten and turn upright. The longer the tree has grown in the bound condition, the harder it will be to straighten and the less perfect will be the results. So it is with people who have lived a lifetime in bondage. God's people are to be trees of righteousness, upright, well-formed and bearing fruit.

It is important for the one receiving ministry that there be an ongoing relationship with a body of believers who can intercede for them, and minister love, acceptance and encouragement. They need a family to relate to and from whom to learn the proper responses to situations as demonstrated by Christ Himself. We as Christians must respond to life's situations as Jesus would. Only then can we raise up healthy children of the Kingdom.

They will know that we are Christians by our love, not by our "gifts" or our knowledge of the Bible. Only when the Bible becomes a living book, manifested in our daily lives by the Spirit of God, Who is love, will it be effective in the world. Love never fails.

To order Destiny Image
or Treasure House books,
please write:

Destiny Image Publishers
P.O. Box 310
Shippensburg, PA 17257

or
call toll free:
1-800-722-6774